ARCHAEOLOGY AND THE
PRE-CHRISTIAN CENTURIES

OTHER PATHWAY BOOKS

BIOGRAPHICAL NOTE

J. A. Thompson attended the University of Queensland and the University of Melbourne, and holds degrees in science, the arts, and theology. For a number of years he taught chemistry and physics. Then in 1947 he became Director of the Australian Institute of Archaeology in Melbourne, where he lectured in the School of Semitic Studies in the University, and in Old Testament and Hebrew in two of the theological colleges. During 1950-51 he was an honorary Fellow of the American Schools of Oriental Research at the Jerusalem school and worked at the archaeological sites of Roman Jericho and Dibon. In 1957 he was appointed Lecturer in Old Testament Studies in the Baptist Theological College of New South Wales.

ARCHAEOLOGY AND THE PRE-CHRISTIAN CENTURIES

by

J. A. THOMPSON

LECTURER IN OLD TESTAMENT STUDIES
BAPTIST THEOLOGICAL COLLEGE
NEW SOUTH WALES, AUSTRALIA

WM. B. EERDMANS PUBLISHING COMPANY
GRAND RAPIDS, MICHIGAN

Library of Congress catalog card number, 58-13061

Printed in the United States of America

Second printing, September 1959

DEDICATION

To my Parents

PREFACE

This book takes up the account of archaeological discoveries bearing on the Old Testament, at the point where it was laid down in the author's previous volume *Archaeology and the Old Testament*. It carries on the story for the post-exilic period up to the days of Herod the Great, but makes no attempt to deal with the valuable New Testament material that is now available. The method followed here is the same as that followed in the former volume. Archaeological evidence is assembled and set in a background of history which, though not given in detail, is sufficient to provide the reader with some general bearings. The material of this second book was omitted in the earlier volume because it is extensive enough to be given a place on its own. Any attempt to include it in the former volume would have minimized the importance of the magnificent archaeological discoveries for both the pre-exilic and the post-exilic periods. In any case there is such a complete break in the history of the people of Palestine at the time of the Exile, that it seems fitting to treat the post-exilic period as a section on its own.

As in the previous volume, the material presented here has been worked out in the classroom situation in theological colleges and Bible colleges, and in the University of Melbourne over the past decade. It is still finding a place in the teaching of the author in the college where he now teaches. This second volume is now sent forth to join its companion in the hope that both may prove a help to students in learning their first lessons in Biblical Archaeology.

The writer acknowledges the help of Dr. L. L. Morris, one of the Consulting Editors of the Pathway Series, who has again read all the manuscripts and made valuable comments. Thanks are due also to Rev. B. G. Wright and to Mr. Victor

Eldridge, both of whom have read the manuscript and given helpful suggestions. Acknowledgment is also gratefully made of help given by the writer's wife, who has undertaken the typing of the material for presentation to the publisher.

J. A. T.

CONTENTS

LIST OF MAPS AND ILLUSTRATIONS

Maps

Illustrations

CHAPTER ONE

DAYS OF EXILE

WHEN THE PEOPLE of Jerusalem went into exile in the days of Nebuchadnezzar, a period of history closed for Israel. The tribal units that had entered Palestine in the time of Joshua had been united under King Saul about 1050 B.C. Following the death of Solomon, the land had been divided into two kingdoms, each of which had gone its own way, and each of which fell in turn before a great conqueror, Israel in 722 B.C. before the Assyrians, and Judah in 586 B.C. before Nebuchadnezzar and the Babylonians (or Chaldeans).

After each disaster, thousands of captives were taken to lands far away from the homeland. We know little of the fate of the exiles from Israel, but we do have some knowledge of the exiles from Judah. It will be our task in this book to piece together the information which has become available from archaeological and historical sources during the past fifty or sixty years, and which bears on the centuries between the collapse of Judah and the birth of Christ.

THE HOME OF THE EXILES IN BABYLONIA

Bible history makes it clear that the people of Judah were invaded more than once by the armies of Nebuchadnezzar. In 597 B.C. King Jehoiachin and many of his notables, among whom was the prophet Ezekiel (Ezek. 1:2), were taken away to Babylonia. When Jerusalem fell to Nebuchadnezzar in 586 B.C. another group of people from Judah joined the party that had been exiled some eleven years before. It is of great interest to us to read the letter that the prophet Jeremiah wrote to these first exiles. Jeremiah stayed behind in Jerusalem and was still there when the city finally fell to the Chaldeans. But he wrote to the first group of exiles words of encouragement, urging them to build houses, plant gardens, take wives, raise children, and pray for the peace of the city to which they had gone (Jer. 29:1-7). All of this argues for a degree of freedom for the exiles in that foreign land.

The first group was already settled in the region of the river Khebar. Thanks to archaeological discovery, the general area where these people lived can now be identified with some certainty. Much of our information comes from the ancient site of Nippur, in southern Mesopotamia, which will be referred to again in this book. This town has been excavated in part, and excavations are still proceeding there. Among the cuneiform tablets discovered in the ruins were two, dating respectively to 443 B.C. and 424 B.C., which refer to a waterway named "naru kabari" or "nehar kebar," which in English is river Khebar.[1] This waterway was evidently an artificial canal which started from the Euphrates River just north of Babylon, and which can be traced further south until it joins the Euphrates again south of Ur of the Chaldees. Nippur itself is some sixty miles southeast of Babylon and the canal flowed through Nippur. There was therefore a connection by water between the general area where the exiles lived and the capital of the great Nebuchadnezzar.

It is interesting to note that the place name Tel Abib (Ezek. 3:15) is a Hebrew adaption of a Babylonian name Til Abubi.[2] The Babylonian words mean "the mound of the flood." The actual site is not known, but it was no doubt one of the many old mounds or tells formed from the debris of ruined cities. These had been long unoccupied and some of them were thought to go back to the days before the great Bible flood. Apparently some of these were resettled. Other similar sites, for example Tel Melah and Tel Harsha (Ezra 2:59, Neh. 7:61), are referred to in the Bible as having been

1. G. A. Cooke, *The Book of Ezekiel*, International Critical Commentary (Edinburgh, 1936), p. 4.
2. *Ibid.*, p. 42.

occupied by the exiled Jews. G. A. Cooke says that the name Tel Abubi was a common name in Babylonia at all periods. It was known in Hammurabi's code and on one of the inscriptions of the Assyrian King Tiglath Pileser.[3]

Actually in the vicinity of Nippur there are several old mounds and, as we shall see later, there is clear evidence that there were Jews living in this area between 500 and 400 B.C.[4] We may conjecture that these later Jews were descendants of the earlier exiles deported from Judah just after 600 B.C.

We can picture the Jewish exiles then, settled in a foreign country among the heathen, and engaged in some sort of forced labor under Nebuchadnezzar. Here they were to dwell for many years until finally many of them returned home just after 540 B. C. as a result of the decree of the conqueror Cyrus. Their lot may not always have been hard, for preachers like Ezekiel were evidently free to preach to the people who seem to have had some sort of limited local government with "elders." Their true condition remains largely a matter of conjecture. F. F. Bruce has made the fascinating suggestion that the exiles were drafted into a forced labor gang working on the Babylonian irrigation system.[5]

BABYLON THE GREAT

The great capital was some 60 miles away from the exiles. Very likely few of them ever saw the great city. Yet it is of some importance for us as Bible students to know something about this city which is described in such glowing terms in several passages in the Bible. Thus the book of Isaiah refers to it as "Babylon, the glory of kingdoms, the beauty of the Chaldees' excellency" (Isa. 13:19).

Babylon was an ancient city with a long history of occupation. Nebuchadnezzar determined to restore and to extend it so as to make it one of the most wonderful of all the cities in the East. In this he succeeded. Today, thanks to the work of

3. *Ibid.*
4. See below p. 66ff.
5. F. F. Bruce, *Bible Study Notes*, Jan.-Feb., 1951, p. 34.

Robert Koldewey and his team of German archaeologists, we have a good idea of the splendor of the city of those days. During the years between 1899 and the first World War, the ruins of the inner city of Babylon were thoroughly excavated. A vast system of fortifications, streets, canals, palaces, and temples was brought to light. Well might Nebuchadnezzar have described this city in the words of Daniel 4:30, "Is not this great Babylon, that I have built for the house of the kingdom [royal dwelling place] by the might of my power, and for the honour of my majesty?"

The inner city where the king had his palaces is seen today as a remarkable complex of ruins. Entrance was gained through the great Ishtar gate, a double gate leading through double fortification walls. It was adorned with magnificent enamelled bricks into which patterns were worked, patterns of flowers, geometrical figures, life-sized animals, bulls, lions, and dragons. The Ishtar gate must have been startling in its beauty. Once inside this magnificent gate, the visitor would pass along the stone-paved procession way in the heart of the city proper. This way was walled up with enamelled bricks decorated with life-sized lions. To the right of the procession way lay the palace area, likewise adorned with beautiful enamelled bricks. One fine room decorated with bricks of gold and blue must have been the throne room. Some writers have made the suggestion that this was the place where the finger wrote on the wall although the Bible does not actually assert this. In the same general area is a strange structure thought by some to be the remains of the famous "Hanging Gardens." Whether or not this particular set of ruins can be identified with this well-known world wonder, it remains true that one of the features of the mighty Babylon was a remarkable set of gardens supported on terraces and thrust up into the air. They were built, according to tradition, for the wife of the king, a woman from the cool mountain regions to the north, so as to give her both beauty and coolness.

Further down the procession way on the right lay the temple area where the priests' quarters as well as the temple

of Marduk, known as Esagila ("house whose top is lofty"),
were to be found. The most spectacular of all the buildings
in the sacred area was the great ziggurat or temple tower which
rose up into the sky in eight stages, according to the Greek
historian Herodotus.[6] There were other notable buildings in
the heart of this splendid city. Outside the main city area were
various fortification walls at intervals of miles apart, all de-
signed to make Babylon impregnable. Truly this was an outstanding city and one to be proud of.

And Nebuchadnezzar was proud indeed as the inscriptions
show. Among the ruins of the city Koldewey found a good
deal of inscribed materials, partly on bricks and stones, and
partly on baked clay tablets. Many of the written records indicate the pride and confidence of Nebuchadnezzar, as a selec-
tion of these inscriptions will show:

> A great wall which like a mountain cannot be moved I made of
> mortar and brick. . . . Its foundation upon the bosom of the abyss
> I placed down deeply . . . its top I raised mountain high. I trip-
> licated the city wall in order to strengthen it. I caused a great
> protecting wall to run at the foot of the wall of burnt brick . . . .[7]
> When Marduk the great lord named me the legitimate son and
> to direct the affairs of the land . . . Babylon his mighty city . . .,
> its great walls I completed. Upon the thresholds of their great
> gates strong bulls of bronze, and terrible serpents ready to strike,
> I placed. That which no king had done my father did in that he
> enclosed the city with two moat-walls of mortar and brick. As
> for me, a third great moat-wall, one against the second. I built
> with mortar and brick, and with the moat-wall of my father
> joined and closely united it. Its foundation upon the bosom of the
> abyss I laid down deeply, its top I raised mountain high . . . .[8]
> The produce of the lands, the products of the mountains, the
> bountiful wealth of the sea, within her I gathered . . . great quan-
> tities of grain beyond measure I stored up in her. At that time
> the palace, my royal abode . . . I rebuilt in Babylon . . . great
> cedars I brought from Labanon, the beautiful forest to roof
> it . . . .[9]

Concerning one of the temples, Nebuchadnezzar spoke in the
following terms:

6. Herodotus, *The Histories* (London, 1954), p. 86.
7. W. H. Lane, *Babylonian Problems* (London, 1923), p. 179.
8. *Ibid.*, p. 178.
9. *Ibid.*, p. 181.

> Huge cedars from Lebanon, their forest with my clean hands I cut down. With radiant gold I overlaid them, with jewels I adorned them . . . the side chapels of the shrine of Nebo, the cedar beams of their roofs I adorned with lustrous silver. Giant bulls I made of bronze work and clothed them with white marble. I adorned them with jewels and placed them upon the threshold of the gate of the shrine . . . .[10]

In contrast to all these grandiose words we listen to the words of the prophets of Israel with something of awe:

> And Babylon, the glory of kingdoms, the beauty of the Chaldees' excellency, shall be as when God overthrew Sodom and Gomorrah. It shall never be inhabited, neither shall it be dwelt in from generation to generation (Isa. 13:19, 20).
> Babylon shall become heaps, a dwellingplace for dragons, an astonishment, and an hissing, without an inhabitant.
> Though Babylon should mount up to heaven, and though she should fortify the height of her strength, yet from me shall spoilers come unto her, saith the Lord.
> Thus saith the Lord of hosts; The broad walls of Babylon shall be utterly broken, and her high gates shall be burned with fire (Jer. 51:37, 53, 58).

Babylon was not beaten down by an enemy. It was taken by the Persians in 539 B. C. and became a sort of second capital. In the days of Alexander the Great it was still occupied, although Alexander undertook the clearing up of certain deserted areas. In Roman times there was a town here. The town, however, was slowly deserted and today the state of ruin of the once magnificent city is a telling commentary on the proud words of the man who made it in his day the wonder of all the East.

ARCHAEOLOGY AND THE PROPHET EZEKIEL

It was during the days of exile that the prophet Ezekiel sought to show the exiles that they were suffering the just consequences of their sins. It has been the traditional view of the Christian Church that the book of Ezekiel should be taken at its face value so that we regard the prophet as having done his preaching during the period 597 to 573 B.C. in the land of Babylonia. More recently there have been those who have

10. *Ibid.*, p. 187.

sought to show that this prophet lived in Palestine for at least part of his ministry. Others have tried to show that the prophecy came from a date much later than the exile. In these discussions archaeology has done a good deal to support the traditional view.

Already we have made reference to some of the place names which are not inconsistent with a Babylonian residence for Ezekiel. Indeed, they require it, if the geographical data are to have meaning. But there are other pointers. In Ezekiel 4:1 the prophet is commanded to take a brick and draw on it a map of Jerusalem. The Hebrew word here refers to a sun-dried brick, and while it was quite usual to draw sketches on such mud bricks in Babylonia,[11] we are not aware that this sort of thing was ever done in Judah. Again, the fact that Ezekiel was commanded to "dig through" the walls of the house as he acted a parable of the removal of people from the doomed city of Jerusalem points to Babylonia (Ezek. 12). Excavations show that the usual medium used for house construction in these lands was mud or adobe. In Palestine, on the other hand, the walls were made of stone, and the act of digging through a wall would invite the collapse of the wall (Ezek. 8:8, 12:5-7) [11a] It has been maintained that walls of mud were non-existent in Palestine in the sixth century B. C. but were in fact the only walls in use in Mesopotamia.[12] Other passages in Ezekiel's prophecy refer to the same type of house. Thus Ezekiel 13: 10-15 refers to a house where the rain storms will wash away the plaster. The same picture of adobe walls in the houses is found in Ezekiel 22:28.

Evidence that Ezekiel wrote at the time of the exile comes from a most unusual source, namely the description of the east gate in the ideal temple described in Ezekiel 40:5ff.[13]

11. Edward Chiera, *They Wrote on Clay* (Chicago, 1938), pp. 160-164.

11a. Mud houses are to be seen, however, in Palestine in some places today.

12. C. C. Howie, *The Date and Composition of Ezekiel* (Pennsylvania, 1950), p. 18.

13. *Ibid.*, pp. 43ff.

There is enough data here for the careful reader to be able to reconstruct the ground plan of the gateway. It turns out to be a gate with provision for three doors, one behind the other, in a space of 25 cubits. Archaeologists point out that this type of gate was of a very old pattern. It was quite common in the days of King Solomon, for example, and is known in excavations at Megiddo, Ezion Geber, and Hazor in the towns that go back to the days of Solomon. Another interesting fact is that this type of gate disappeared in the ancient eastern scene in the ninth century B. C. and was replaced by a new style of gate altogether. A certain number of the older type of gate must have remained in use for years after their construction, but sooner or later they would all disappear, so that by Ezekiel's day it would be almost impossible to find one. How then would Ezekiel in a vision see a gate, the like of which was known in Solomon's day, but which had long since gone out of use in the East? The answer is that he must have seen the Solomonic gate in the Temple in Jerusalem prior to its destruction by Nebuchadnezzar in 587 B.C.[13a] The destruction of the Temple would have removed what was probably the last gate of this kind to be seen in the East. In any case, here is a reasonable explanation of why Ezekiel would see such a gate in his vision, and incidentally a reason for thinking that he lived at the time of the exile.

There is another possible link with Babylonia, which, although not accepted by all commentators, seems to the present writer to have some value. It is that the strange imagery in Ezekiel 1 owes something to the Babylonian environment. In his vision, Ezekiel saw strange creatures with human heads and wings, and in the imagery we hear of the face of a man, a lion, an ox, and an eagle (Ezek. 1:5-11). The partly human, partly animal forms are reminiscent of the guardian figures

13a. The size of the gate described in Ezekiel 40 is not significant because it is in any case visionary. It is the pattern that concerns us. There is little point to argue as some have done that the size of Ezekiel's doorway would have been too big for the temple known in Solomon's time and still standing in Ezekiel's earlier years.

of the Babylonian temples, which may have been known to Ezekiel. It is quite within the range of the facts of Biblical history and also of our own experience today, that God takes up the events and experiences of life as a starting point for speaking His mind to us. It was the storm that gathered on that day that was the prelude to God's revelation to Ezekiel. The storm was merely an attendant on God's throne. So, too, God called on the visual impressions so familiar to Ezekiel to grant to him a vision of the divine splendor.

SOME LATER MILITARY EXPLOITS OF NEBUCHADNEZZAR

Bible readers are familiar with those military events that concern the fall of Jerusalem. We referred in our earliei book[14] to the recent publication of an important document which refers to the campaign of Nebuchadnezzar in 598 B.C. which led to the captivity of Jehoiachin (II Kings 24:10-16). Reference has also been made to the valuable receipts from Babylon which refer to the presence of Jehoiachin here in 592. Unfortunately, written evidence of the campaigns of Nebuchadnezzar is sparse at present. That he had other campaigns is certain, and some of these are referred to in the Bible. Thus he had dealings with both Tyre and Egypt. Ezekiel 29:18 speaks of his siege of Tyre, but we still await archaeological evidence of this event. Concerning Egypt, however, we have one inscription which, though far from complete, does tell of a campaign in that land.[15] The prophet Ezekiel spoke of the judgment God intended for Egypt at the hands of the Babylonian king in several places (Ezek. 29:19, 30:10, 32:11). A fragmentary historical text dating from the 37th year of Nebuchadnezzar, which is the year 567 B.C., speaks of fighting between Pharaoh Amasis and the king of Babylon. Unfortunately the tablet is so badly damaged that we can draw little reliable information from it. It may have been confined to the

14. J. A. Thompson, *Archaeology and the Old Testament* (Grand Rapids, 1957), p. 114.
15. J. B. Pritchard, *Ancient Near Eastern Texts* (Princeton, 1955), p. 308.

area of the Delta only, [16] and again we await further archaeological light. By this date Nebuchadnezzar was already old and his days of fighting were over.

A further tantalizing inscription from these days refers to an expedition to the general area of Syria and Lebanon.[17] This, too, however, is incomplete and lacks definite evidence as to the date and the occasion. What interests us is that the prophet Ezekiel infers that for many years after the fall of Jerusalem the Babylonians were active militarily. It is Babylon that is to be the agent of divine judgment on Tyre and Egypt. The inscriptions, though meager in number and content, do at least point to a continuation of the campaigns of the great king for a number of years. We live in hope that yet further excavation will bring to light additional significant evidence about these times which are so vital in Bible history.

THE CLOSING YEARS OF CHALDEAN POWER

When Nebuchadnezzar died in 562 B. C. after a reign of forty-two years, he was followed in quick succession by three weak kings; first by his son Amel Marduk (562-560 B. C.), whom Jeremiah calls Evil Merodach (Jer. 52:31, II Kings 25:27), then by Nergal-shar-usur (Neriglissar), one of the nobles and son-in-law of Nebuchadnezzar who replaced the inefficient Amel Marduk in a revolution and reigned from 560 to 556, and finally by the weak son of this last king, Labashi Marduk, who was replaced by a second revolution a few months after he came to the throne. One of the conspirators, Nabonidus (Nabunaid), then ruled as the last king of Babylon (556-539).

The names of these three kings are known in written records. Thus Neriglissar's name appears on contract tablets as early as 596 B. C. Apart from Evil Merodach, who according to the Bible released King Jehoiachin (II Kings 25:27), we have no special interest in these rulers. The last king of Babylon is,

16. There are useful discussions in H. L. Ellison, *Ezekiel* (Grand Rapids, 1958), p. 102, and H. R. Hall, *The Ancient History of the Near East*, (London, 1950), p. 549.

17. J. B. Pritchard, *op. cit.*, p. 307.

however, of very real interest to us, for it was in his time that the collapse of Babylon became imminent.

Nabonidus ascended the throne amid bloodshed. Already the people of the land had shown considerable discontent with the Chaldean rulers and in two revolutions had managed to replace them. The new ruler was a man of culture with such a keen interest in antiquity that he has been described as the world's first archaeologist. He restored the Temple of the Moon in Harran where his mother was probably a priestess. Perhaps he was in fact a Syrian, and from the outset he stood little chance of gaining popular approval. But he took steps at once to make an impression on the people. An important basalt stela, now preserved in Istanbul, tells of his rise to power.[18] He declared:

> I am the real executor of the wills of Nebuchadnezzar and Neriglissar, my royal predecessors. Their armies are entrusted to me and I shall not treat carelessly their orders . . . .

Referring to the previous king he declared that

> Labashi Marduk, a minor who had not yet learned how to behave, sat on the royal throne against the intention of the gods.[19]

The inscription goes on to tell how one night in a dream Nebuchadnezzar and his attendant appeared to Nabonidus on Marduk's command, to interpret strange signs in the heavens as a portent of a long reign. Other gods, too, sent favorable signs. It is evident from the inscription that the new king wished to indicate to the people that he had the personal approval of both Marduk the god, and the former Nebuchadnezzar.

Important new inscriptions from Haran were found in 1956[18a] during an examination of the mosque which now stands on the old site. Three basalt stelae about two metres high by about a metre wide had been found and re-used in the mosque, but they were ancient and carried cuneiform inscriptions re-

18. *Ibid.*, p. 309.
18a. These documents have been published by C. J. Gadd in *Anatolian Studies*, Vol. VIII.
19. *Ibid.*

lating to the days of Nabonidus. Two of these tell of the reign of this ruler and of his restoration of the temple of the moon goddess Sin at Haran. Nabonidus said that it was Sin "who called him to kingship." It would seem, however, that he earned the hostility of the people for his support of Sin, and it may have been partly for this reason that he retired to Teima for several years. The third stela is an account of the life of Nabonidus' mother who was a votaress of the moon goddess.

In an attempt to win the esteem of the priests Nabonidus undertook various works of restoration in the temples of Babylonia. He richly endowed many of these, restored the temple of Marduk in Babylon, and journeyed through the land, bestowing gifts on the gods of each sacred shrine: Sin at Ur, Shamash at Larsa, Ishtar at Uruk. Before long, however, he offended the priests greatly and paved the way for his own downfall. The year after his accession he was called to the west to quell a revolt. Moving on to Hamath and turning south towards Edom, he discovered the oasis at Teima where he settled down, to remain till perhaps his sixteenth year. This was a fatal mistake, for it was necessary for the king to be present each New Year in Babylon for the special annual procession of the gods. In his absence the procession could not be held. It was an occasion when pilgrims flocked to the great city and when the coffers of the temples profited greatly. As the king stayed away year after year, the anger of the priests grew.

Back home in the capital the king appointed his son Belshazzar to be the actual ruler. One cuneiform inscription reads as follows:

> He entrusted a camp to his eldest, first-born son; the troops of the land he sent with him. He freed his hand; he entrusted the kingship to him. Then he himself undertook a distant campaign, the power of the land of Akkad advanced with him; toward Teima in the midst of the westland he set his face . . . . He slew the prince of Teima . . . then he himself established his dwelling in Teima . . . .[20]

20. Quoted in J. Finegan, *Light from the Ancient Past* (Princeton, 1947), pp. 189-190.

The important Nabonidus Chronicle[21] issued later in all probability at the inspiration of Cyrus, makes the point that in the seventh, ninth, tenth, eleventh years "the king was in the city of Teima. The son of the king, the princes and his troops were in Akkad . . . ." More important is the repeated statement that "the king did not come to Babylon for the ceremony of the month of Nisan."

It is interesting to comment here that since it was Belshazzar who exercised the co-regency in Babylon, and probably did so to the end, the book of Daniel is not wrong in representing him as the last king of Babylon (Dan. 5:30). A man like Daniel who was honored would thus be "third" in the kingdom.[22] Incidentally, the reference in Daniel 5:18 to Nebuchadnezzar as "father" of the king may simply follow Semitic usage which allows language like this in the case of family relationships, or it may follow on the claims of Nabonidus that he was the legitimate heir of Nebuchadnezzar.

The days of Babylon were drawing to a close. Further to the east a petty king, Cyrus the Persian, had in a remarkable way become ruler of both Media and Persia and had embarked on a program of expansion. In 546 B. C. he had conquered Lydia. In the following years he was able to bring most of the East under his control leaving only Babylonia as a last pocket of resistance. These ominous events led to some action on the part of Nabonidus. The Nabonidus Chronicle tells us that the king was still at Teima in the eleventh year, that is, 546 B. C. He may have stayed there longer, for the Chronicle has a gap at this point and does not resume till the seventeenth year, which was the last year of his reign. There must have been something of a panic, for the record tells us that "Bel went in procession," that is, the New Year festival was held. Moreover, the gods from neighboring cities were entering Babylon. We think that in a vain hope to gain some protection from them, Nabonidus gathered gods into Babylon. Some

21. J. B. Pritchard, *op. cit.*, p. 305.
22. The Aramaic word means literally "Third" but it came to mean, more generally, a prominent officer of state.

cities resisted this summary carrying off of their gods to Babylon, if we are to judge from the Chronicle: "The gods from Borsippa, Kutha . . . and Sippar did not enter."[23]

In October 539 Babylon fell to the Persians. There were battles in the outskirts of Babylon some days before. On the fourteenth day Sippar was seized and "on the sixteenth day Gobryas ['Ugbaru] the governor of Gutium and the army of Cyrus entered Babylon without battle. Afterwards Nabonidus was arrested in Babylon when he returned there."[24]

The end of the two co-rulers Nabonidus and Belshazzar was death at the hands of the Persians. A new age had dawned for the people of the East and in particular for the Jews in exile. It was to usher in days of return and restoration.

ARCHAEOLOGY AND THE PROPHET DANIEL

We do not intend here to enter the lists and fight a battle with the literary critics about the date of this important book in the Old Testament. That decision rests on a number of considerations. There are, however, a number of comments that may be made from the archaeological angle, for undoubtedly the author of this book was reliably informed on a number of issues. In particular the fifth chapter has a number of items which suggest a well-informed writer.

The references in various places in this book of Daniel to soothsayers, magicians, astrologers, and the like (Dan. 1:20, 2:10, 4:7, 5:11, etc.), are all authentic items in the background of the times. Excavations have produced a good deal of material about the religion of Babylon, and it is clear that magic and divination played a large part.

Another feature of the book of Daniel which has an authentic ring is the great importance attached to dreams. We have already noticed how Nabonidus made a strong point of the dream in which he saw Nebuchadnezzar. Dreams figure in the authentic records of Mesopotamia from the earliest times,

23. J. B. Pritchard, *op. cit.*, p. 306.
24. *Ibid.*

forming an integral part of the kings' actual accounts of their own reigns.[25] It is quite wrong to write off all dreams as apocryphal accretions. Even if ancient rulers invented the dreams, they were accepted by the people as one of the ways in which the gods spoke to men. Hence the many references to dreams in the context of Babylonia are quite in keeping with the facts of the case.

Up to the present the enigmatic figure of "Darius the Mede" of Daniel (5:31, 6:1ff., 9:1, 11:1) is quite unknown to the archaeologist. Concerning this man W. F. Albright wrote,[26] "The elusive problem of Darius the Mede remains exactly as puzzling as ever; it certainly cannot be solved merely by hyper-criticism." Perhaps we have to do here with a title.

One of the texts of Nabonidus found at Haran[26a] and dated to 546 B.C. refers to the "King of the Medes." This statement opens up the whole question afresh. D. J. Wiseman[26b] asks whether this phrase may not have been another name for Cyrus. Certainly the people of Haran spoke of the king of the Medes in 546 B.C. But by this time there was no such king, his place having been taken by Cyrus the Persian who went on to conquer Babylon. Wiseman suggests that we should translate Daniel 6:29 as "in the reign of Darius, even in the reign of Cyrus the Persian."

We have already referred to the place of Belshazzar in the closing days of the Chaldean rule in Babylon. The writer was correctly informed in this matter. The relationships between Nabonidus and his son and the achievements of each have been made the subject of a valuable piece of research by R. P. Doughtery in his book, *Nabonidus and Belshazzar*,[27] which contains a wealth of valuable material about these times.

25. Cyrus Gordon, *Introduction to Old Testament Times* (Ventor, 1953), pp. 66-67.
26. W. F. Albright, *Journal of Biblical Literature*, Dec. 1949, p. 375.
26a. See pp. 21, 22.
26b. D. J. Wiseman in *Documents from Old Testament Times* (London, 1958), ed. Winton Thomas.
27. R. P. Dougherty, *Nabonidus and Belshazzar* (Yale, 1929).

The story of the three young men who were thrown into a fire because they refused to worship the image of the king (Dan. 3) reminds us of the large brick kilns outside the city where Nebuchadnezzar's workmen baked bricks for his buildings. Some of these have been uncovered in excavations. A strange comparison with this very incident comes from the days of Rim Sin, a former king in these lands (1750 B. C.). This king once decreed concerning four men of Larsa:

> Because they threw a young slave into an oven, throw ye a slave into a furnace.

Although the precise significance of the decree is not clear, E. G. Kraeling remarks about this incident, "Clearly, that sort of thing was nothing new in Babylonia."[28]

While these items do not settle the date of composition of the book of Daniel they show that the author was in possession of a good deal of authentic background material. Archaeological research can do much to establish the value of the background material appearing in an ancient document such as this.

THE EXILES LOOK HOMEWARD

Ezekiel the prophet had spoken of days of restoration and had told the people of his vision of the valley of dry bones (Ezek. 37). Earlier still the prophet Jeremiah had spoken of restoration after seventy years (Jer. 25:12) under the kings of Babylon. Magnificent passages in the latter part of the book of Isaiah gave strong hope of restoration. Here, too, Cyrus was referred to as the Lord's shepherd, the Lord's anointed (Isa. 44:28, 45:1). As the years went by, and more especially as the progress of Cyrus the Persian was witnessed, there must have been a spirit of keen anticipation among those exiles who still held to the faith of their fathers. The Lord was about to turn again the captivity of Zion (Ps. 126). No longer need the exiles sit down and weep by the waters of Babylon (Ps. 137). To the exciting story of Cyrus and his decrees which granted freedom to all exiles, we now turn.

28. E. G. Kraeling, *Bible Atlas* (Chicago, 1956), p. 323.

CHAPTER TWO

THE RETURN OF THE JEWS FROM EXILE

———————

THE FALL OF BABYLON in 539 B.C. ushered in twenty-five years of significant history for the Jews. After the restoration of their Temple in 516 B.C. or early 515 B.C. we enter upon a period of comparative silence. But these early days were vital in setting the pattern for a good deal of the subsequent history of the Jews. In actual fact considerable numbers of the exiles did not return from Babylonia and those who did were faced with tremendous hardships in their own land. There were droughts, there were enemies on every hand, the land to which the Jews were returning had been devastated and required much attention before it would yield the fruits of the field, and finally heavy taxation was exacted by the Persian overlords. By perhaps March 515 B. C. the Temple was completed in Jerusalem. This gave to the returning exiles a tangible focal point in their national life. There is quite an amount of archaeological material referring to these days, far more indeed than there is for the subsequent centuries.

THE DECREES OF CYRUS

The book of Ezra opens with an account of the decree of Cyrus which allowed the exiles to return to their land:

> Thus saith Cyrus king of Persia, The Lord God of heaven hath given me all the kingdoms of the earth; and he hath charged me to build him an house at Jerusalem, which is in Judah. Who is there among you of all his people? his God be with him, and let him go up to Jerusalem, which is in Judah, and build the house of

the Lord God of Israel, (he is the God,) which is in Jerusalem (Ezra 1:2-3).

There is an alternative form of this decree in Ezra 6:3-5.

Historians of a former day approached these simple Biblical statements with suspicion.[1] Some writers argued that we had no evidence that Cyrus made a decree of this kind, much less that he paid any sort of honor to the God of Israel. He was a Persian who worshipped Persian gods and could hardly be expected to pay honor to the God of the Jews. We no longer raise questions of this kind since we have given due weight to important documents from the days of Cyrus which show us that he was a master of propaganda and knew how to exploit every occasion to the best advantage for himself. A study of the so-called Nabonidus Chronicle, of the famous Cyrus Cylinder, and of the verse account of Nabonidus, helps a great deal in understanding the true state of affairs at the time.

The Nabonidus Chronicle referred to in our previous chapter[2] was almost certainly prepared under the direction of Cyrus. We have seen how it tells us of the last years of Nabonidus and of how he neglected his duties to the gods in Babylon. It is clear that Nabonidus in a last panic gathered many gods into Babylon as a sort of protection in his time of desperation. It was all to no avail. The Chronicle tells us that the noble Cyrus was welcomed into the city with real joy.

> In the month of Arahshamnu, the 3rd day, Cyrus entered Babylon, green twigs were spread in front of him . . . the state of Peace was imposed upon the city . . . . From the month of Kislimu to the month of Addaru, the gods of Akkad which Nabonidus had made come down to Babylon . . . returned to their sacred cities . . . .[3]

It is evident from this document that Cyrus had a policy of returning the gods to their own homes. This fact is borne out by a study of the important Cyrus Cylinder which was specially

1. W. O. E. Oesterley and T. H. Robinson, *A History of Israel*, Vol. II (Oxford, 1932), pp. 75, 81.
2. See above. p. 22. See also J. B. Pritchard, *Ancient Near Eastern Texts* (Princeton, 1955), p. 305.
3. *Ibid.*, p. 306, col. 2.

prepared for the occasion. The document which is really a baked clay cylinder, begins with a strong piece of propaganda in which the new king shows how he has the approval of the gods. After some broken lines in the record it goes on to say:[4]

> . . . the correct images of the gods he removed from their thrones, imitations he ordered to place upon them . . . . he interrupted in a fiendish way the regular offerings . . . . the worship of Marduk, the king of the gods, he changed into an abomination, daily he used to do evil against his city . . . . Upon their complaints the lord of the gods became terribly angry . . . . he scanned and looked through all countries, searching for a righteous ruler willing to lead him [Marduk] in the annual procession. Then he pronounced the name of Cyrus, king of Anshan, declared him to become the ruler of all the world . . . . Marduk the great lord, protector of his people, beheld with pleasure his [Cyrus'] good deeds and his upright mind and ordered him to march against Babylon.

This must have been of tremendous value in establishing the prestige of the new king in the eyes of the Babylonians. Here then was the legitimate king of the region, who had the approval of the gods. Cyrus wisely entered Babylon without destroying the city, and gave careful instructions to his troops to respect the people and their property. The story is told in considerable detail on the cylinder. More was needed, however, in order to secure the goodwill of the people, and especially of those who were slaves in that land. It would be wisdom indeed to free all captives and restore them to their homes. This Cyrus did. The decree reads:[5]

> As to the inhabitants of Babylon who against the will of the gods . . . . I abolished the corvee [yoke] which was against their social standing. I brought relief to their dilapidated houses, putting an end to their main complaints

It is not hard to see in these words the intention of the king that enslaved peoples should be freed, although it must be admitted that these words might have applied only to the local Babylonians. Later on in the document, however, we have a

4. *Ibid.*, p. 315, col. 2.
5. *Ibid.*, p. 316, col. 1.

possible reference to the return of exiles of various kinds to their lands:[6]

> I also gathered all their former inhabitants and returned to them their habitations.

As to the treatment of the gods we have some clear statements. The gods were to be returned to their homes and restored to their temples which were to be repaired:

> I returned to the sacred cities on the other side of the Tigris, the sanctuaries of which have been ruins for a long time, the images which used to live therein and established for them permanent sanctuaries. I also gathered all their former inhabitants and returned to them their former habitations. Furthermore I resettled on the command of Marduk, the great lord, all the gods of Sumer and Akkad whom Nabonidus has brought into Babylon . . . . May all the gods whom I have resettled in their sacred cities daily ask Bel and Nebo for a long life for me . . . .[7]

It was clearly the policy of the Persian ruler to allow freedom of worship. It is to be noticed that although Cyrus was not a worshipper of the gods of Babylon he knew how to make a show of honoring them in order to win his way with the Babylonian people. We need not conclude that because he spoke in terms such as we read in this document that he necessarily worshipped the gods of Babylon.

In the light of material like this we may conclude that Cyrus prepared similar documents for other people. In the case of the Jews there were no images to be restored to the Temple, but there was a Temple to be rebuilt and sacred vessels to be returned. It is sheer hyperskepticism to deny that Cyrus granted to the Jews privileges similar to those that were allowed to other people. We argue that the brief decrees in the book of Ezra are extracts from longer decrees issued for the Jews by the great king. We need not pay particular attention to the fact that Cyrus seems to pay honor to the God of the Jews. He probably paid no more respect or worship to this God than he did to others.

6. *Ibid.*, p. 316, col. 2.
7. *Ibid.*, p. 316.

That Cyrus did in fact restore temples is borne out by some of the inscriptions found in excavations. Thus, at Uruk[8] the German excavations showed that the sanctuary of Ishtar was rebuilt by Cyrus who left inscribed bricks on which this claim was made. At Ur[9] also, although inscribed bricks show that some restoration was done by the former ruler Nabonidus, it is of special interest to us to find that Cyrus himself authorized and completed a great deal of restorative work in the sanctuaries of Ur. Both inscribed bricks and an important baked clay cylinder found near to the great ziggurat refer to this fact.

Further information along this line is obtained from a baked clay tablet in the British Museum,[10] unfortunately badly damaged, which presents in verse form the information contained in the Nabonidus Chronicle. We now know it as the "Verse Account of Nabonidus." It was evidently prepared by the priests of Babylon, and gives in panegyric form an account of the victories of Cyrus. Despite the gaps we can still read that Cyrus, after the capture of Babylon, was occupied with sacred works. He multiplied the offerings to the gods and prostrated himself before them. He restored the gods and the goddesses to their sanctuaries and sent back the people with them.

There can be no doubt that Cyrus showed a great deal of tolerance towards the various religious sections in the community. It is against the background of these facts that we must read the decrees of Cyrus found in the Bible. Quite clearly there is every reason to regard the Biblical accounts as authentic. W. F. Albright has written, "The substantial historicity of the Edict of Cyrus in 538 has been confirmed by modern archaeological discoveries."[11]

One further point is relevant to our discussion. The two accounts of the decree of Cyrus in the Bible are in two different languages. The passage in Ezra 1:2-4 is in Hebrew, and the passage in Ezra 6:3-5 is in Aramaic. This fact may well be

8. R. P. R. de Vaux, "Les Décrets de Cyrus et de Darius sur la reconstruction du Temple," *Revue Biblique*, Jan. 1937, p. 33.
9. *Ibid.*, p. 34.
10. J. B. Prichard, *op. cit.*, pp. 312-315.
11. W. F. Albright, *The Biblical Period* (Oxford, 1952), p. 49.

significant because on the one hand Persians used Aramaic in their official and international documents, and on the other hand it seems clear that they often used the local languages for the promulgation of information in given areas. In Ezra 6:2 there is a specific term used, *dikronah,* which we now know to have been an Aramaic term for an official memorandum "which recorded an oral decision of the king or other official and which initiated administrative action. It was never intended for publication but solely for the eye of the proper official, following which it was filed away in government archives."[12] This will explain why the document was later found in the official archives at Achmetha or Ecbatana (Ezra 6:2).

The Hebrew document of Ezra, chapter 1, would refer to information for local national consumption. It was a proclamation in Hebrew, to be made possibly by the royal heralds, and it was addressed to those who claimed to be worshippers of Yahweh, God of heaven. Precisely the same sort of thing happened elsewhere in Persian times as we know today from documents brought to light by the archaeologists in which the wishes of the Persian king were made known to the people in written form, in their own tongue. For example, there are records from Egypt, not precisely from the days of Cyrus, but from the days of his successor Darius, who instructed the Egyptians in matters affecting their religion. He sent a message to the satraps (governors) of Egypt to assemble the wise men, priests, and scribes to undertake the publication of the ancient laws of Egypt, as they affected in particular the Pharaoh, the temples, and the people. Again, there are inscriptions in the local Egyptian script referring to the work of Darius in restoring temples and the like.[13] There are also several references to the beneficent acts of the Persian kings in the general area of Asia Minor. The name of these rulers was long remembered in these areas, and one notable inscription found near to Magnesia in Asia Minor, written in Greek, refers to a letter

12. G. E. Wright, *Biblical Archaeology* (Londan, 1957), p. 200.
13. R. P. R. de Vaux, "Les Décrets de Cyrus et de Darius sur la recontruction du Temple," *Revue Biblique,* Jan. 1937, p. 40.

from Darius to his local satrap expressing grief that damage has been done to his reputation because the satrap had charged impost on sacred vessels of the god Apollo. These cases point to the possible use of local scripts and writings in certain cases where the Persian king wished to express his will.

In the light of all this evidence there seems no reason to doubt that the decrees of Cyrus recorded in the Bible give the substance of the originals. In any case, much of the background we have been able to discover from archaeological research lends support to the Biblical picture. Thus it was that Jews who lived in Babylonia found themselves in the year 539 B. C. in the happy position of being able, if they so desired, to return to the land of their fathers.

THE LAND OF JUDAH AT THE TIME OF THE RETURN

It has been pointed out more than once in recent years that at the time of Nebuchadnezzar's final assault on Judah in the years 587-586 B. C., there was considerable destruction in all the cities of Judah. W. F. Albright has written in this connection:[14]

> A fair number of towns and fortresses of Judah have now been excavated in whole or in part; many other sites have been carefully examined to determine the approximate date of their last destruction. The results are uniform and conclusive: many towns were destroyed at the beginning of the sixth century B. C. and never again occupied; others were destroyed at that time and partly reoccupied at some later date; still others were destroyed and reoccupied after a long period of abandonment, marked by a sharp change of stratum and by intervening indications of use for non-urban purposes. There is not a single case known where a town of Judah proper was continuously occupied through the exilic period.

The destruction does not seem to have extended to the former territory of Israel. North of Jerusalem we have evidence, based on excavations, that towns were occupied there throughout the sixth century. In particular the town of Bethel,

14. W. F. Albright, *Archaeology of Palestine* (London, 1956), pp. 141-142.

DAYS OF THE PERSIANS

(The earlier kingdoms are also shown)

which really lay outside Judah proper, in the area of Benjamin, was occupied till about 500 B. C. when it was destroyed. The reason for its destruction is still unknown. Further north, towns like Samaria, Megiddo, and Tell en Nasbeh, whose Biblical name is not now known, were all occupied in the sixth century. All of this points to the fact that Nebuchadnezzar confined his destruction to the area of Judah, although, as the quotation from Albright shows, he ravaged that land thoroughly.

It seems evident, therefore, that when the Jews returned from their exile, they returned to a land that had little in the way of towns, houses, or farms awaiting them. It has been suggested that only one other period in the history of the land showed such a tragic picture, and that was before the days of Abraham, at the close of the Early Bronze Age.

The actual area occupied by the returning Jews was a small one. Its limits can be partly worked out from the material supplied in the lists given in Ezra 2 or in Nehemiah 7. It extended from Bethzur, which is just north of Hebron, to a point not far north of Jerusalem, perhaps twenty-five miles from north to south along the central ridge. Nehemiah 7:66ff. gives a population of just under 50,000.

Were it not for the generous attitude of Cyrus and his successors we may well wonder how the returning Jews survived. Hostile neighbors were likely to cause trouble, and the burden of a land which had lain waste now for over half a century was a big one. It was to this task that the returning exiles now set their hands.

A BRIEF REVIEW OF THE KINGS OF PERSIA UP TO 500 B. C.

In order to obtain a correct perspective for our study, we should now give some attention to the story of the Persian rulers and their methods of government during these years, since these facts are important for our understanding of the Biblical narrative.

The first of these rulers was Cyrus. Already in 549 B. C. he had united the peoples of Media and Persia under his rule and by 546 he had subdued Croesus the king of Lydia. In 539 B.C. he entered Babylon, which he was to rule till 530 B.C. We think of him today as the founder of the great Persian Empire. In order to govern his great domain he established twenty provinces called satrapies, each ruled by a satrap (protector of the kingdom). These officers were kept under his eye by means of his personal secretaries, financial officers, and generals, who owed allegiance directly to him, although they served in the capitals of the satraps. The vast expenses of such an empire were raised from taxation which was often unkind. This taxation was to be a source of trouble to the people in Judea, who, as subjects of the Persian rulers, had to pay their share. There are Biblical references to this burden of taxation as, for example, in Nehemiah 5:4.

In the year 530 B. C. the great Cyrus was killed in battle fighting some tribal peoples to the northeast of his land. His son Cambyses rescued his body and buried him in a tomb that was already prepared and which can be seen today, although it has since been plundered.

Cambyses had helped his father to govern Babylon and was an experienced ruler. During his short reign he was able to conquer Egypt, and by 525 Memphis the capital of Egypt was in his hands. We remember this king in Jewish history because of his kindness to the Jewish settlement away down the Nile at Elephantine. Here there was a military post manned by Jews to protect the southern borders of the land. We have no idea of the origin of the Jews here, but they had some sort of a temple erected for worship. When Cambyses destroyed the local temples of the Egyptians he spared the temple of the Jews, a fact which is mentioned in important documents from a later day to which we shall refer later.[15] When the task was completed in Egypt, Cambyses set out on the return journey. As he reached Mount Carmel in Palestine, he heard that a usurper had risen up in Persia and claimed his throne.

15. See below p. 68ff. See also J. B. Pritchard, *op. cit.*, pp. 491, 492.

Whether due to shock or, as some claim, by his own hand,[16] he died there.

In the service of Cambyses was a younger relative, Darius by name. He left Palestine at once and organized opposition to the usurper. Before the year 522 had passed, the usurper, Bardiya, whose real name was Gaumata, was slain.[16a] Meantime, revolts broke out all over the empire and Darius began a struggle for recognition. After two years he was able to subdue all his opponents and rule supreme. He commemorated his success by having a mountainside smoothed off and a huge inscription carved on its face, with a picture of himself placing his foot on the head of one of his conquered foes. This inscription is still to be seen at Behistun. Darius had a long reign, lasting till 486 B.C., during which he did much to reform the laws of Persia and to extend his domains. It was he who built the first canal to join the Mediterranean Sea to the Red Sea.[17] He also undertook the invasion of Greece but was defeated at the battle of Marathon, in 490 B. C. His work as a builder is seen in palaces from his time which have been excavated in Babylon, Susa, and Persepolis, although his successors extended his building program considerably. Finally, we remember him as an outstanding financier who standardized the weights and measures of Persia, developed the coinage, which in his day was of comparatively recent invention,[18] and began to interfere in the commercial life of the people. Some economists say that owing to the government interference price levels rose with a jump at the start of the reign of Darius and contributed in the end to the economic disintegration of the great empire.[19] Numerous documents of the period found in excavations show the extent to which the king was taking an

16. Herodotus, iii, 62f.

16a. The original Bardiya was a brother of Cambyses but was executed for rebellion. Gaumata, a Magian, claimed to be this Bardiya whose death was never announced.

17. A. T. Olmstead, *History of the Persian Empire* (Chicago, 1948), p. 145.

18. F. A. Banks, *Coins of Bible Days* (New York, 1955). p. 15. A. T. Olmstead, *op. cit.,* (Chicago, 1948), pp. 186-87.

19. A. T. Olmstead, *op. cit.,* pp. 193-94.

undue share of the profits of the traders.[20]   This led to price
rises and to the distress of the poor people.   We have traces of
this trouble in the Bible, for example, in Nehemiah 5:1-4.

THE RETURN OF THE EXILES

The Bible has two lists which give the composition of the
group that finally left Babylonia to return to Judea, one in
Ezra 2 and one in Nehemiah 7.   These lists differ slightly from
one another, and various attempts are made to explain this.
Many writers are inclined to think that the lists refer to the
state of affairs at the time when the story in Ezra and Nehemiah was finally committed to writing.[21]   More recent study
has sought to show that the difference between the two lists
can be explained best in terms of slight scribal variations in
lists which were compiled from an actual original which made
use of a numerical notation such as we have found in several
Aramaic documents from Persian times.   This system of notation which was widely used both among the Persians and also
among the later Nabataean and Palmyrene scribes consisted
of a series of strokes and other special marks which could lead
to minor scribal variants.   It is suggested that the Jews themselves had a similar system and, indeed, there is a hint of this
on some of the ostraca from Samaria dating back to the eighth
century B. C.   A recent writer on this subject has said:[22]

> As for the lists in Nehemiah 7 and Ezra 2, while at first glance
> these textual numerical differences may seem detrimental, act-
> ually they greatly enhance the value of the lists, as they bring
> out much of their real nature and age — remains of ancient
> census lists made by the builders and supporters of the restora-
> tion and reform sometimes called 'the Second Temple,' docu-
> ments vested with reality and antiquity by the very blemishes
> and signs of use they exhibit.

20. *Ibid.*
21. W. F. Albright, *The Biblical Period* (Oxford, 1952), p. 62,
Note 122.
22. H. L. Allrik, "The Lists of Zerubbabel (Nehemiah 7 and
Ezra 2) and the Hebrew Numeral Notation," *Bulletin of the
American Schools of Oriental Research*, Dec. 1954, p. 27.

It seems clear that the returning company of Jews wished to remain exclusive and required that a man should have his name on the official list before he could gain recognition in the community. For this reason many of the local people were excluded (Ezra 4:1, 2).

It is evident from documents unearthed at Nippur,[23] that many Jews did not return at this time. Those that did were led by Shesh-bazzar (Ezra 1:8, 11). This man had a Babylonian name, perhaps Sin-ab-usur or Shamash-ab-usur, but there is some dispute as to who he was. There is a name like this among the sons of Jehoiachin (Jeconiah) in the list in I Chronicles 3:17-18, Shenazar, and it has been thought that the strangeness of the name caused scribal confusion. It was not at all impossible that in 538 B.C. there should be a son of Jehoiachin alive. He had five sons in 592 B.C. according to tablets found in Babylon,[24] and they could not have been very old at the time of the return. There may well have been a son still alive aged sixty or so.

On the other hand, some writers[25] have held that we may have here a Babylonian official in Persian employ to whom was entrusted the task of leading the Jews home. Another Persian official, Mithredath, handed to him the sacred vessels of the Temple (Ezra 1:8), and presently the party set out for their homeland. In the subsequent story, the Bible tells us only of the work of Zerubbabel (Zer-babil, offspring of Babylon) and Jeshua the priest. What happened to Shesh-bazzar we do not know. Perhaps he was frustrated by the groups that later troubled Nehemiah, or perhaps his task was only of limited duration and having completed it he returned to Persia. In any case, Zerubbabel and Jeshua alone feature in the Bible story.

This Zerubbabel had a Babylonian name but he was the son of Jehoiachin's eldest son Shealtiel. It was these two

23. G. E. Wright, *Biblical Archaeology* (London, 1957), pp. 205-6.
24. J. B. Pritchard. *Ancient Near Eastern Texts* (Princeton, 1955) p. 308, col. 2.
25. E. G. Kraeling, *Bible Atlas* (Chicago, 1956), p. 329.

men, Zerubbabel and Jeshua, who led the national life. Although the first aim was to build a Temple, they were sidetracked and did little about it till the days of Darius.[26] They seem to have done some preliminary work and to have made arrangements to obtain cedar logs from Tyre. Just here we can add an archaeological note. Ezra 3:7 refers to cedar trees being brought by sea to Joppa. It is of real interest to us today to learn that there was a town at the mouth of the little Yarkon River in those days, originally founded about 1200 B. C., but still in use in Persian times. Today it is known as Tell Qasile. It was excavated in part in 1948-1950.[27]

When the time was ripe to take up again the building of the Temple, it was Zerubbabel who was to the fore. In the exciting days that followed the death of Cambyses, the prophets Haggai and Zechariah called on this man, who is described as "governor of Judah" (Hag. 1:1ff.), or as "the Tirshatha" (Ezra 2:63), a Persian word meaning "his excellency," and known from Persian documents of those days. Haggai gave his first message in August 520 and called on Zerubbabel to commence work on the Temple. The foundation was laid and the work put in hand. At once there were local objections from Tattenai, governor of the province "beyond the River."

This governor is known in a document from Babylon dating from a few years later, actually 502 B. C.[28] The name is also known from a text referring to "Tattenai prefect of Susa."[29] This latter is not the man in the Bible, but the text shows that the name was a common one in those times. E. G. Kraeling has suggested that the name Tattenai may have been confused with Ushtanni, who is known in Babylonian texts as governor of "Babylon and beyond the River" and whose first recorded date is March 21, 520 B. C.[30]

26. The writer is well aware of the many unsolved problems about the foundation of the Temple.

27. B. Maisler. "The Excavation of Tell Qasile," *The Biblical Archaeologist*, May, 1951, pp. 43ff.

28. E. G. Kraeling, *op. cit.*, p. 331.

29. *Ibid.*

30. *Ibid.*

The objections of Tattenai led to the search for the original memorandum of Cyrus to which we have already referred.[31] This was found in the archives at Ecbatana (the Biblical Achmetha, Ezra 6:2). Permission being granted to continue, the work went on and was finally completed in March 515 B. C. (Ezra 6:15). Some have seen in the willingness of Darius to accede to the request of the Jews a desire on his part to win over yet another part of his domains. The work of the prophets Haggai and Zechariah fell at the time when Darius was just recovering from the revolts of recent days. Perhaps indeed Zerubbabel was a loyal supporter of the new king at first. There is more than a hint, however, that he allowed himself to become the center of hopes for the restoration of the throne of David (Haggai 2:20f. and Zech. 4:6, 7; 6:12, 13; etc.).[32] The opinion of W. F. Albright is of interest:[33]

> Haggai's second oracle . . . exults in the approaching downfall of Persia and the coming of a new Jewish state; in his fourth oracle (Hag. 2:20ff.) dated in December, while the Babylonian rebellion still appeared to be successful, he explicitly declared that the imperial throne would be overturned and implied that Zerubbabel was the Lord's anointed . . . . Whether Zerubbabel died a natural death or was removed, we cannot say; there is not the slightest reason to suppose that he committed any overt act of disloyalty to the crown . . . . evidently the Persian authorities contented themselves with depriving the Davidic family of its political prerogatives, which were turned over to Joshua and his successors. We may safely credit Joshua with political astuteness in the difficult situation in which he found himself.

Unfortunately we have no archaeological evidence about the Temple. If there are remains today they lie beneath the present ground level. The whole Temple area has suffered greatly through the centuries, and while no doubt there would be much to bring to light if the archaeologists could only excavate on the site where the great Mohammendan mosque now

31. See above p. 32.
32. The prophecies were made in all sincerity and under divine inspiration, but some change in conditions must have led to the postponement of God's purposes. See Jeremiah 18:6-10, for an important principle.
33. W. F. Albright, *The Biblical Period* (Oxford, 1952), p. 50.

lies, we must await the future before we can discover what lies buried there.

It is significant that the state of Judah seems to have been ruled internally by the high priests from this time onwards. We know quite a number of the high priests between these days and New Testament times. Perhaps for political purposes the Persians appointed governors, but they seem to have allowed the normal internal affairs of state, like taxation, to be supervised by the high priests. That the Persians did allow some sort of priestly rule in their empire is shown by the fact that the priests of Hierapolis in northern Syria were able to levy their own taxes and strike their own coins.[34]

THE PROVINCE OF JUDAH IN 500 B. C.

It is evident, then, that the little province of Judah was closely linked with the great Persian administration from the time of Cyrus onwards. In political status it was only a small part of a much larger satrapy. We have seen that the Persians organized their vast domains into large units called satrapies which were ruled by satraps. Persian inscriptions like the great biograhy of Darius on the rock at Behistun list these satrapies. A. T. Olmstead in his *History of Persia* refers to other lists at various periods in Persian history which make it possible to trace changes in the disposition of these satrapies. Many of these satraps replaced former kings and became little monarchs themselves, and for this reason the Persian authorities needed to keep them in check. These larger units were then divided into smaller provinces each with its own administrator. One of these satrapies defined by Herodotus as the fifth, "Beyond the River [Trans-potamia],"[35] seems to have been subdivided into several provinces, among them being Judah, Samaria, Ammon, Ashdod, and Arabia. The province of Judah was surrounded by these others, whose governors quite naturally viewed any sign of expansion with suspicion.

34. *Ibid.*, p. 55.
35. Herodotus, iii, 89ff.

The complete satrapy thus included Syria, Palestine and other areas to the west of the Euphrates, all united into the one large area of "Babylon and Ebir-nari [across the river]."[36] We know some of the satraps who ruled this vast area, men like Gobryas and Ushtani (or Hystanes). A. T. Olmstead describes the position of Zerubbabel in this complex system as "only a governor of the third rank." His immediate superior was Tattenai, governor of Across the River, who in turn was under the authority of Hystanes, satrap of "Babylon and Across the River."[37] In later years following a revolt in Babylon in 482 B. C. the satrapy of "Across the River" was detached from Babylon. This was the state of affairs when Nehemiah was governor, and we must take up the point again later.

At the end of the sixth century B. C. we must picture a little province under the control of the returned exiles, protected by royal decree, but surrounded by hostile neighbors, and opposed even by those Jews who had never gone into exile but who had stayed in the general area to which the exiles returned.

36. A. T. Olmstead, *op. cit.*, pp. 56f.
37. *Ibid.*, pp. 138-39.

CHAPTER THREE

THE PERSIAN PERIOD IN PALESTINE FROM 500 B. C. TO 330 B. C.

AFTER THE BUILDING of the Temple the Jews entered on a period of history which is for us today obscure to say the least of it. The darkness is penetrated at one or two points only, notably in the days of the governor Nehemiah who rebuilt the wall of Jerusalem. A certain amount of material is available from excavations in towns that were occupied in Palestine during Persian times and from these we gain some insight into the types of buildings in use, the pottery, the coinage and in particular the growing influence of Greek culture in the land. But we have no clear idea of the way in which the Persians ruled the land for we know of only two governors of these times, Nehemiah and Bagoses, although we have some reason to think that the priests did a good deal of the routine work of government, notably in the area of tax-collection. Modern archaeological work gives some insight into the neighboring peoples who feature in the Biblical narrative. Outside of Palestine we know something about the Jews in Mesopotamia and Egypt, and we shall devote a special chapter to these groups, but it would be well first of all to review the history of the Persians during the period 500 B. C. to 330 B.C. This will provide a good background against which to view the story of the Jews as far as we can reconstruct it today.

PERSIAN KINGS FROM 500 B.C. TO 330 B. C.

At the close of the sixth century B.C. the great Darius was still ruling and was to continue till 486 B.C. We have referred to his attack on Greece and to his defeat at Marathon in 490 B.C. His achievements were great indeed and his successor Xerxes I (486-465 B.C.) who had been trained in the art of government, by being allowed to rule as viceroy in Babylon, carried on his work. In the light of this experience he was able at a later date to carry through some vital administrative changes in government. His father had commenced to build several great palaces, perhaps the most notable of all being that at Persepolis, but it was left to Xerxes to bring the whole magnificent plan to completion, and to change it in certain respects. He alone seems to have been responsible for the magnificent reliefs which surpass all the earlier work of his father's craftsmen. He had many military successes in all parts of his own empire despite the fact that he did suffer defeat at the hands of the Greeks in the battles of Thermopylae and Salamis in 480 B.C. and again at Plataea the next year. Perhaps in actual fact these successes of the Greeks were not so great as subsequent Greek writers made them out to be, but they did arouse Greek patriotism and had a tremendous effect on the morale of the Greeks. We know Xerxes best in Biblical history from the story of Esther, which took place in the old Elamite town of Susa, conquered by Cyrus, but at the time of the Bibical story the site of a beautiful palace built by Darius, and later enlarged and completed by Xerxes. That this monarch lived there for at least some of his reign is evidenced by documents found in Susa [1] although there were other palaces, the best loved of them being that at Persepolis.

The next king was Artaxerxes I (465-424 B.C.) during whose reign the famous Nehemiah was governor of Judah, and Ezra the scribe was active.[2] Important documents from Egypt and Mesopotamia dating partly from the reign of Artaxerxes and partly from the reign of his successor Darius II (423-404

1. A. T. Olmstead, *The History of the Persian Empire* (Chicago, 1948), pp. 230-231 and pp. 266-267.

2. The writer is not unaware of the proplem of Ezra but holds that Ezra and Nehemiah were contemporary. See below pp. 47, 48.

B.C.) [3], give us evidence about the Jews for these years. There was a brief period of two years between these two kings, during which Xerxes II (424-423 B.C.) occupied the throne, but this king is relatively unimportant.

The last four kings were Artaxerxes II (404-358 B.C.), Artaxerxes III (358-338 B.C.), Arses (338-336 B.C.), and Darius III (336-331 B.C.) Persia collapsed finally before the Greek invader Alexander the Great in 331 B.C.

ARCHAEOLOGY AND THE BOOK OF ESTHER

The little book of Esther is placed in the days of Xerxes whose Biblical name is Ahasuerus. It is a puzzling book in some ways because it is difficult to identify most of the people concerned from external evidence. The chief characters of the book, Vashti, Haman, and Mordecai are unknown in non-Biblical history. Excavations, however, as well as general historical evidence make it clear that there is much in the book that shows the writer to have been correctly informed on many of the background details of the story.

Xerxes (Ahasuerus) was a historical person. The picture given in the book of Esther of a king who was a despot and thoroughly sensuous in character corresponds with the account given by the Greek historian Herodotus.[4] He greatly enlarged his harem at Persepolis as excavation shows,[5] and became involved in a shameful affair with his brother's wife and later the daughter as well.

The description of the ornate palace with its bright curtains is quite in the manner of the gaudy palaces of the Persians. Excavations at Susa (Biblical Shushan) have yielded abundant evidence of the rich ornamentation of the walls of the palace and of the richly colored glazed bricks used there.[6]

3. Some Egyptian documents come from the reigns of Darius I and Xerxes I as well. See below p. 71.
4. Herodotus, *The Histories* (London, 1955), pp. 594-96, or Herodotus ix, 107ff.
5. A. T. Olmstead, *op. cit.*, Chapter 20.
6. *Ibid.*, pp. 166-171. Also R. Ghirshman, *Iran* (London, 1954), pp. 165-167.

This palace, commenced by Darius, was described in glowing terms. It was built of special timbers and adorned with gold, lapis lazuli, turquoise, silver, and ebony, and was erected by men who came from all over the empire.[7]

The story of Esther could well fit into the time of Xerxes for he reigned for twenty years, and the events of this book do not go beyond the twelfth or possibly the thirteenth year (Esther 3:7, 12). The banquet in the third year may coincide with the great council that Xerxes held before the invasion of Greece, and the four years that intervened before Esther became queen may well fit into the time that the king was absent in Greece (Esther 1:3, 2:16).[8] The standard commentaries on the book of Esther point out that many of the customs referred to in the story are quite in keeping with Persian practice.[9] Thus the arrangements for the banquet (1:6-8), obeisance before the king and his favorites (3:2), belief in lucky and unlucky days (3:7), exclusion of mourning garb from the palace (4:2), hanging as the death penalty (5:14), dressing a royal benefactor in the king's robes (6:8), dispatching couriers with royal messages (3:13, 8:10), are all customs that are now well known from the written records that have come to light.[10] There are, moreover, a good number of Persian words in the book, largely from the language of government and trade. All of these facts show that, at the very least, the author of the book of Esther was well informed on numerous matters of Persian practice and Persian life, and while there are difficulties of interpretation and identification still remaining, we may hope to find yet more archaeological evidence to clear up the historical situation. It is risky to adopt the view that has been adopted by many modern writers, that the whole story is pure fiction, especially when we have to argue so much from silence, a very uncertain basis for argument in any case.

7. R. Ghirshman, *op. cit.*, pp. 165-166.
8. *Herodotus* vii, 8.
9. For example, L. B. Paton, *The Book of Esther*, International Critical Commentary (Edinburgh, 1951), pp. 64ff.
10. *Ibid.*, p. 65.

EZRA THE SCRIBE

The date at which Ezra did his work is not clearly specified in the Bible, which merely says that it was in the seventh year of Artaxerxes the king (Ezra 7:7, 8). The question immediately arises as to whether this was the first or the second king of this name. If it was the first, the date would be 458 B.C., but if it was the second it would be 397 B.C. The Bible certainly gives us the impression that Ezra preceded Nehemiah. There is little in the way of archaeological evidence to help us solve the question of dating. This is in striking contrast to the case for Nehemiah where we have convincing evidence for a date of 444 B.C. One possible reconstruction which allows of Ezra preceding Nehemiah, and which appeals to the present writer, is as follows.

Artaxerxes I in his seventh year, following the practice of other Persian kings, decided to investigate the religious condition of the Jews in Judah. Such inquiries were not unusual and there is in existence today an important document from Egypt which tells of a similar inquiry into the religious observances of the Jews in Egypt towards the end of the fifth century B.C.[11] In the present instance, Ezra, a Jew living in Persia, was selected by Artaxerxes I because of his reputation in matters of Jewish law, and he was given a strict commission to go to Judah and inquire concerning the way the people obeyed the law of their God. He was to take free-will offerings from the Jews in his own land and have access to government funds if he needed extra money. After inquiry, he was to teach the ignorant, and then enforce the law with penalties (Ezra 7:11-26). He duly arrived in Judah and delivered his commission to the local rulers.

About the same time some illegal building was being carried on in Jerusalem and a complaint went to the king that a wall was being built around the city (Ezra 4:11-16). A prayer recorded from the lips of Ezra makes reference to God giving

---

11. J. B. Pritchard, *Ancient Near Eastern Texts* (Princeton, 1955), p. 491.

Above:

Painting by Maurice Bardin of construction, according to Unger, Babylon (see pp. 13ff.).

Below:

The Ishtar Gate and adjacent ruins of ancient Babylon (see p. 14).

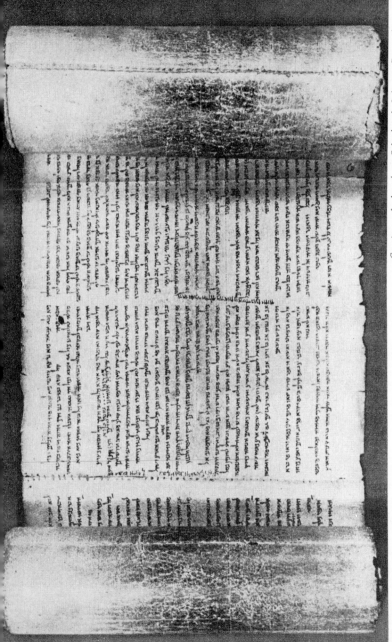

The Roll of Isaiah found in 1947 in a cave near the Dead Sea (see p. 103).

the people a wall in Judah and in Jerusalem (Ezra 9:9). The
next we know is that Artaxerxes had forbidden the building
of a wall and the work of Ezra was cut short. Ezra did indeed
attempt some reforms, but little attention is paid to these in
the record and we may conjecture that not much was achieved.
Perhaps Ezra was disgraced and his commission taken away
because he became involved in the matter. It is here suggested
that he went into retirement to reappear when Nehemiah
came as governor. If this is not the true picture, then we have
to place Ezra after Nehemiah, or at least allow that Nehemiah
preceded him to Judah and that he followed a little later.
This is the view taken by W. F. Albright,[12] who holds that
Ezra came in the thirty-seventh year of Artaxerxes. The fact
is, however, that we lack external evidence of an archaeological
kind to solve the problem.

NEHEMIAH THE GOVERNOR AND RESTORER OF THE WALLS OF JERUSALEM

At first reading of the Biblical records we are in a similar
quandary about the date of Nehemiah, for the start of his story
is in the twentieth year of Artaxerxes. Now is this the first
or the second king of this name? The discovery of Aramaic
documents at Elephantine[13] in Egypt has placed it beyond all
doubt that it is the first of these kings that is referred to in
the Bible. The details of this argument will be given in the
next chapter, and for the present we shall accept the fact.

It was late in 445 B. C. that Nehemiah learned from his
brother Hanani and other Jews who had come from Jerusalem
that the situation there was bad. The lack of a wall made
attacks from hostile neighbors inevitable. At the time there
was a ban on the building of the wall (Ezra 4:17ff.). By careful pleading, Nehemiah was able to have this order reversed
and was himself appointed governor of Judah (Neh. 5:14).
Provided with letters to the governors of "Beyond the River,"

12. W. F. Albright, *The Biblical Period* (Oxford, 1952), pp. 53, 64.
13. For detailed discussion, see Chapter 4, below.

a Persian province (Neh. 2:7, 9), and with a military escort, Nehemiah set out for Judah. Three days after his arrival he went by night on a tour around the city walls. The account of this journey in chapter 2:12-15, together with the accounts of the walls in chapters 3 and 12:31-40, makes a striking picture when compared with the reports of excavations conducted at various points around the walls in recent times. While it is not possible to sort out the picture completely, the disposition of the places mentioned on the eastern side of the city is fairly well agreed upon today. One recent writer has said:[14]

> The topographical texts of Nehemiah are likewise of exceptional value, even more so than any passages in Josephus, not only because they present us with a thrice repeated wall description by an eye witness more detailed than that of Josephus (Neh. 2:11ff., 3, 12:31ff.), but especially because they deal with the city of the Old Testament itself, before as well as after the Exile. When Nehemiah arrived in Jerusalem Herod's extensive levelling and enlargement operations in the sacred quarter were still far off.

It is true that there is some discussion going on about the exact site of the Valley Gate and the whole matter hinges on whether the pre-exilic city included the southwestern hill.[15] This can only be decided after more excavation. The writers of two large works on Jerusalem in recent years, L. G. Vincent and J. Simons, both include the southwestern hill in the pre-exilic city. A good discussion of the minimal view of the walls has recently been given by M. Avi-Yonah in the *Israel Exploration Journal*.[16] In certain areas it has been possible to understand some of the features brought to light in the excavations by reference to the Biblical narrative. Captain Weill, excavating in the southeast corner of the city, revealed a remarkable staircase which was evidently set in a sort of postern gate in the wall. The Bible reference to Nehemiah's procession at this point reads:

14. J. Simons, *Jerusalem in the Old Testament* (Leiden, 1952) pp. 437-38.
15. E. G. Kraeling, *Bible Atlas* (Chicago, 1956), p. 336.
16. M. Avi-Yonah, "The Walls of Nehemiah — A Minimalist View," *Israel Exploration Journal*, vol. IV, 1954, pp. 239f.

> And at the fountain gate, which was over against them, they
> went up by the stairs of the city of David (Neh. 12:37).

This seems to suit the staircase revealed in the excavation,
since the stairs ran between two walls which joined the main
outer wall at right angles and then led up into the heart of
the city of David. In this same area Charles Warren in 1867
found evidence for a tower, perhaps the tower of Nehemiah
3:25-27.

An opening in the wall here has been taken to be the Foun-
tain Gate. J. Simons has written:[17]

> The real importance and practical value of Nehemiah's wall
> descriptions consist first of all in the fact that to them we owe
> the knowledge of a very considerable number of features, espe-
> cially on and near the city's fortified perimeter, which are not
> mentioned even in passing by any other Biblical writer and these
> features are so numerous that without them our picture of bib-
> lical Jerusalem would lose half or more than half of its contents.
> The Dung Gate, the "Mishneh" Gate, the Water Gate, the In-
> spection Gate, the Fountain Gate, and the Sheep Gate would all
> be entirely unknown to us but for the texts of Nehemiah .... The
> same would be true as regards the Tower of the Furnaces, the
> "wall of the square," the "wall of the pool of Shiloah," the
> "stairs of the city of David" and several features connected with
> the water supply, e.g., the Dragon Well and the King's Pool.

Now the fact that a number of these features has been discovered in excavations leads us to believe that if ever extensive
digging can again be carried out all around the area where the
walls once ran, we shall find the descriptions of Nehemiah
most valuable in interpreting the discoveries.

The Biblical narrative tells of the completion of the work of
rebuilding, a task in which men from various areas played a
part. Perhaps the towns referred to in chapter 3, which makes
reference to the men of Tekoa, Beth-zur, Keilah, Zanoah, Jerusalem, Gibeon, Mizpah, Jericho, and Beth-haccerem, give us
the best idea we have of the extent of Judah at the time. By
placing these on a map, it is possible to see at a glance the
area from which Nehemiah drew his helpers.

17. J. Simons, *op. cit.*, p. 44.

ARCHAEOLOGICAL LIGHT ON JUDAH'S NEIGHBORS

As Nehemiah began his task, he was greatly troubled by the opposition of various neighbors. The most troublesome of these were Sanballat the Horonite, Tobiah the Ammonite, and Geshem the Arab (Neh. 2:10, 19; 4:1, 3, 7; 6:2; etc.) who plotted against Nehemiah but he was able to frustrate them (Neh. 2:19, 20; 4:6).

Archaeological discovery in this century has produced evidence about these neighbors and in the case of Sanballat and Geshem has brought to light some actual written evidence. The name of Sanballat is now known on one of the Elephantine papyri dating to the year 407 B. C., which can be shown quite clearly to be later than Nehemiah.[18] We shall see that Sanballat had a long life and remained governor in Samaria some years after Nehemiah ceased to be governor in Judah. The name Sanballat is probably a Babylonian name, Sin-uballit. The man was governor of Samaria under Persian overlordship, but almost certainly he was not a Babylonian. The names of his sons Delaiah and Shelemiah are Hebrew, not Babylonian. Both names include the element IAH, which stood for Yahweh, the name of the God of the people of Israel. It is, however, possible, and even likely, that Sanballat followed a syncretistic kind of religion not unlike the religion of the Jews in Egypt. The Elephantine documents, to be discussed in detail in the next chapter, show us that there were other groups who followed a syncretistic religion not unlike that of the Jews.

The name Geshem is now known from two sources, one being a contemporary inscription found at Hegra in Arabia, and the other found in a temple on the borders of Egypt, belonging probably to Arabs who worshipped there at a time when their influence extended to this point.

At the time of Nehemiah the kings of Dedan were the rulers of a vast area to the east of the Jordan and extending away to the south, and although naturally under Persian domination

18. See below, pp. 77, 78.

they had some sort of control over a wide area. They left behind them a variety of inscriptions, one of which reads as
follows:[19]

> Niran, son of Hadiru, inscribed his name in the days of Gashm,
> son of Shahar, and Abd, governor of Dedan.

The phrase "Abd [servant], governor of Dedan" is reminiscent of the one in the Bible, "Tobiah, the servant, the Ammonite" (Neh. 2:10, 19). Tobiah is described as "the servant,"
and the governor of Dedan is "servant." Another feature
about the inscription is the use of the word PHT for *governor*.
This same word occurs in the books of Ezra and Nehemiah as
an element in a proper name, Patah Moab.[20] W. F. Albright
has suggested that the name, which means "governor of Moab,"
may well have come from such a governor, who gave his name
to the family. The word *Patah* would not have been correct
until the time of the Babylonians or Persians, since Moab had
its own tributary kings till at least 645 B.C.[21] These facts, quite
apart from the name Geshem, point to a Persian date for the
inscriptions of Hegra.

Until very recently this reference stood alone, but now we
have some most valuable confirmatory evidence from the Arab
temple referred to above. On the outskirts of the area controlled by the kings of Dedan there was a temple where offerings were made to the North Arabian goddess Han-'Allat,
and in which worshippers had deposited long ago a number
of silver vessels three of which bore inscriptions in Aramaic.
The proper names on these are, with one exception, all north
Arabic. One of them is of special interest to us because it
carries the words

> Qainu son of Geshem (Gusham) king of Kedar.

These inscriptions are securely dated to the end of the fifth
century B.C. by converging lines of evidence. Professor I. Rabi-

19. A. T. Olmstead, *op. cit.*, p. 295.
20. Ezra 2:6, 8:4, 10:30; Neh. 3:11, 7:11, 10:14. Compare W. F.
Albright, *The Biblical Period*, p. 64, note 131.
21. W. F. Albright, *loc. cit.*

nowitz who published the material traces the objects to the Arab shrine at Tell el-Maskhutah (ancient Succoth) in the Wadi Tumilat on the eastern part of the Nile Delta.[22]

It is becoming increasingly evident that the Arab kingdom ruled over by Geshem was quite considerable and included northern Arabia, old Edom, the Sinai area, and part of the Nile Delta, with possibly even a part of southern Judah, where small altars very like those found in southern Arabia have been discovered.[23] This large Arab kingdom was brought under some sort of Persian control and added to the satrap of "Across the River," but its local ruler was evidently allowed to continue as the Persian governor, probably on condition that he paid annual tribute. The discovery in such a context of an inscription such as that we have quoted points with some certainty to the son of the Biblical Geshem.

The third of Nehemiah's troublesome neighbors was Tobiah the Ammonite. While we have no direct evidence of this man at present, we do know quite a deal about his family. His very name suggests that he worshipped Yahweh because of the element IAH at the end. His family was of political importance in Transjordan from the fifth century to the second century at least. At the important site of 'Araq el Emir in central Transjordan, there are some fine rock-cut tombs,[24] one of which bears the name *Tobiah* deeply cut in the rock, in Aramaic letters of the third century B. C. used during the rule of the Ptolemies in Egypt. In the same region we find the remains of what some writers call a palace and others a mausoleum,[25] built evidently by the last of the Tobiad rulers. Earlier on in the third century B.C. we know of an Ammonite governor of this family, because of a letter which he wrote to an Egyptian official named Zeno employed in the government

22. F. M. Cross, "Geshem the Arab, Enemy of Nehemiah," *Biblical Archaeologist*, May 1955, p. 47.

23. W. F. Albright, *Archaeology of Palestine* (London, 1956), pp. 143-44.

24. *Ibid.*, p. 149.

25. G. E. Wright, *Biblical Archaeology* (London, 1957), p. 204. Cf. W. F. Albright, *op. cit.*, pp. 149-150.

of Ptolemy II, Philadelphus (285-246 B. C.). The letter stated that Tubias (Tobiah) was sending to Ptolemy a number of animals including horses, dogs, and camels.[26]

While therefore there is no direct evidence at present for the Tobiah of Nehemiah's day, it is clear that there was a Tobiah family in Transjordan in the centuries that followed, and we have good reason to link these later Tobiahs with the man of Nehemiah's time.

SOME ITEMS OF GENERAL CULTURE

Excavations in Palestine have produced a variety of items of general culture which make their contribution to our understanding of these centuries.

We refer first of all to the pottery of the period. There is a distinctive type of pottery for this so-called Persian or Iron III period, as there is for all archaeological periods. But what is of special interest to us is that at this period a good deal of very distinctive Greek pottery appeared in Palestine, bearing witness to the growing influence of the Greeks in the eastern Mediterranean lands. It was during the sixth century B.C. that the Athenian and other Greek potters set out to master the art of representing the human figure and its drapery in great detail on their pottery pieces. At first they perfected the art of working black figures on to a red background, using a technique that itself was old but was now brought to perfection. About 530 B. C. a new technique appeared in which the potters represented figures in red on a lustrous black background. The Athenians held their art as a sort of a secret and they attained a brilliance in their vases not equaled elsewhere.

The black-figure ware which has been found in many lands in the east, including Egypt, Syria, and Palestine, argues for Greek trading at some time before 500 B. C. There is also a good deal of red-figure ware now known from excavations, showing that the Greeks were active as traders from the fifth

26. G. E. Wright, *op. cit.*, p. 204. See also R. P. L. H. Vincent "La Palestine dans les papyrus ptolémaïque de Gerza." *Revue Biblique,* April, 1920, pp. 161ff.

century onwards. Actually, once the trading began, it continued on through the centuries, the Greek traders being only the precursors of the Greek conquerors. The excavator of the site of Tell en Nasbeh to the north of Jerusalem has written concerning the presence of Greek pottery in this town as follows:[27]

> In a small hill town, even if it was, or had been, the capital of the minute Persian province of Judah, the presence of such ware is significant, telling of close commercial relations between Attica and Palestine in the period of Athens' greatest glory.

In all, some thirty sherds of Greek pottery consisting largely of Attic black-figure ware, although there was some red-figure ware, were found in this excavation. Greek traders evidently visited this town before 500 B. C.

As we turn to coinage we have further significant material. Coinage as we know it today was probably first used by the kings of Lydia when Croesus, their most famous king, stopped minting lumps of so-called white gold about 550 B. C. and changed over to pure gold coinage. The kings of Persia took the lead from here, and Lydian coins served as patterns for the coinage of Persia. On the golden daric and the silver shekel of the Medes and the Persians appeared the picture of the great king. The Greek colonies of the Ionian isles and of Italy copied the idea, and not long after, Greek traders in the eastern Mediterranean started to make coins. The men of old Greece soon followed suit, although they used silver for their coins because they lacked gold. Significant emblems were used on the coins by many of the Greek States. Aegina had a turtle, and Athens, the home of beautiful vases, had a vase. Later, when the Athenian dictator Peisistratus came on the scene, he used the head of the patron goddess of Athens, Athene, on the front of the coins, and a small owl and a twig of olives on the back. The Athenians thought that Athene appeared at times in the guise of an owl, and so they associated this bird with the goddess. The Greek coins were minted in multiples of the drachma.

27. C. C. McCown, *Tell en Nasbeh I* (Baltimore, 1947), p. 62.

Both of these latter facts about Greek coinage, namely, that they were minted in multiples of the drachma and that they carried the picture of an owl, are important for our study of the coinage of Palestine in these times. Coins began to appear in Palestine in the fifth century B. C. and excavations reveal that by the third century they had become abundant. W. F. Albright has noted that[28]

> Silver coins, struck in imitation of Attic drachmas, but with the Hebrew or Aramaic inscription *Yehud*, "Judah," are being found in increasing numbers.

In the same discussion this writer obesrves,[29]

> We have hinted above at the importance of the Attic currency, which became the standard medium of exchange in Palestine more than a century and a quarter before the Macedonian conquest. Attic coins were locally imitated in the second half of the fifth century, and in the following century we find all sorts of barbaric modifications of the figures on the drachma, the owl of Athena being kept until it became unrecognisable.

In the light of these facts it becomes of real interest to discover that several passages in the books of Ezra and Nehemiah referring to events in the latter half of the fifth century B. C., show that the gifts to the Temple were assessed in terms of coins of some kind (Ezra 2:69, 8:27; Neh. 7:70-72). On any system of dating Ezra and Nehemiah, these passages fit into the fifth century B. C., by which time the drachma standard had already penetrated into other lands besides Greece. It is true that there has been some discussion about the exact nature of this coinage, and the Hebrew word *darkemon* has been variously interpreted as *drachma* or *daric*.[30] In either case, these two standards of coinage were in use at the time, and either would suit the Biblical passages.

It is evident from these considerations that the Persians must have granted considerable local autonomy to the Jews, with the right to strike their own coinage. This was not a unique

28. W. F. Albright, *Archaeology of Palestine* (London, 1956), p. 143.
29. W. F. Albright, *ibid.*, p. 143.
30. Compare G. E. Wright, *op. cit.*, p. 203, and W. F. Albright, *loc. cit.*

occurrence, for we know today that the priests of Atargatis at Heliopolis in northern Syria received permission to strike their own coinage and to levy their own temple taxes.[31]

Light on the Persian system of taxation comes from a most unusual source. In order to carry out its tremendous program of government, the Persians worked out an elaborate fiscal scheme, and taxation was levied in all parts of the empire. We gain a brief glimpse into this program in Nehemiah, chapter 5, where we learn that people in Palestine had to mortgage their property in order to meet the requirements of the government. When we come to investigate the methods of collecting taxes, we find light from the seal impressions left on the handles of large jars dating from the fifth and fourth centuries B.C. There are several kinds of seals now known. One type consists of three consonants, YHD, in ancient Hebrew script, together with a small circle in which there is often a cross. This last sign is known from Egypt where it is associated with the letters *lmlk,* meaning "belonging to the king." It was evidently associated in Egypt with some official collection for the king. The letters YHD on the seals found in Palestine signify "Judah," and it is a reasonable conclusion that if at Elephantine in Egypt the symbol of a circle and a cross was associated with the king's portion, it was so in Judah also.

Another group of seals has a circle, inside of which is a five-pointed star, between the points of which are the letters YRShLM, which would spell out *Jerusalem,* in Hebrew. The writing is again in the old type of Hebrew script. A third group of seals written in a more clearly Aramaic script had only the letters YHD on an oval seal without any decoration. Finally, there is a group of seals mostly from Tell en Nasbeh which carry the three letters MTsH, referring possibly to the town of Mizpah.[32] This was evidently an important town in

31. W. F. Albright, *loc. cit.*
32. As an abbreviation. See G. E. Wright, *op. cit.,* p. 203; also H. L. Ginsberg, *Bulletin of the American Schools of Oriental Research,* No. 109, pp. 20f.; N. Avigad, "New light on the MSH seal impressions," *Israel Exploration Journal,* Vol. 8, pp. 113ff.

Persian times, for the text in Nehemiah 3:7 may be translated "Mizpah, belonging to the throne of the governor of this side of the River." The town apparently had some official connection with the satrap of the whole area.

The jar stamps have been found in various places. J. D. Duncan found twenty of them at Ophel (Jerusalem), others were found at Gezer, some twenty-eight others at Tell en Nasbeh. The existence of such a variety of these stamps on the handles of large jars bearing the names of Judah, Jerusalem, and possibly Mizpah, suggests very strongly that there was in use some sort of local method of collecting taxes in kind. Potters were evidently required to make certain jars of standard capacity for the collection of the king's portion.

When we turn to architecture and to building remains of the Persian period left behind in Palestine, we are not very well off. The most spectacular of these is a building at Lachish, on the summit of the mound, which dates from the late fifth, or early fourth century, and which according to several opinions has a number of features that are reminiscent of Parthian buildings in Mesopotamia.[33] Certain new features in architecture are to be found here, suggesting that the ideas were imported from further east. It has been conjectured that we have here one of the residences of the Arab kingdom of which the most famous Biblical representative was Geshem.[34] Certainly Lachish was rebuilt in the fifth century, at a time when the Jews were hardly in a position to build so far to the south. Near to the structure was a small temple that was not destroyed till the second century, probably when the Jews conquered the area. This adds support to the idea that the building may have been an Arab palace. It is further to be noticed that in the same general area of southern Palestine, at the ancient site now known as Tell Jemmeh on the edge of the Negeb, and also at Gezer in the plains of Sharon, small cubelike limestone altars resembling those found in southern

33. W. F. Albright, *Archaeology of Palestine* (London, 1956), p. 145.
34. G. E. Wright, *op. cit.*, pp. 203-204.

Arabia were excavated. It is possible that these came in through trade, but quite likely also that there was Arab control in these areas at this time.[35]

Some beautiful works of art have been found in some sites. Sir Flinders Petrie discovered a tomb at Tell el Far'ah in the Negeb which contained a beautiful silver bowl and a dipper, the latter having for a handle the figure of an undraped maiden.[36]   Art of this kind is known in other parts of the Persian Empire.   Other finds of bronze figures of gods and animals bear witness to the well-developed art of the period in some places.   The art may not, however, have been the work of the Jews themselves, since they normally refrained from representing the form of men and animals in any way at all.

LIGHT ON JUDAH UNDER DARIUS II

Nehemiah left Judah to return to the king in 433 B. C., although he was to return later and continue his work as governor.   We do not know how long he continued in this post, but possibly with the death of Artaxerxes in 423 B.C. he may have been replaced.   He was able to carry out reforms and persuade the people to enter into a covenant with God (Neh. 10), in which, among other things, the people agreed to pay an annual contribution to the upkeep of the Temple (Neh. 10:32).   The same sort of undertaking seems to have held at Elephantine in Egypt where there was a list of those who contributed to the temple upkeep.   The idea was, of course, very old in Israel, going back to Moses' time.

From the days of Darius II (423-404 B. C.) we have some interesting material on the state of affairs in Judah, with the names of some of the significant people who lived at the time. The information comes from the Aramaic papyri of Elephantine and carries our story down to the close of the fifth century B. C.   Before the next century had closed the Persians were overthrown and the Greeks were in the ascendancy.   We

35. W. F. Albright, *Archaeology of Palestine,* pp. 143-144.
36. *Ibid.,* p. 145.

are now in a position to turn to the fortunes of the Jews in lands outside Palestine, and to study this remarkable documentary evidence that has been brought out of the earth by the modern excavator, in both Mesopotamia and Egypt.

CHAPTER FOUR

THE JEWS OUTSIDE PALESTINE IN THE FIFTH CENTURY B. C.

THERE WERE MANY JEWS living outside of Palestine in the fifth century B. C., partly as a result of enforced exile and partly because of voluntary migration. We know of several occasions in Bible history when the people of Israel were taken into captivity. Even before the collapse of the northern kingdom in 722 B. C. there were captives taken from the Galilee area by Tiglath Pileser (II Kings 15:29). When Samaria fell, a further group of exiles was taken (II Kings 17). In the case of Judah, King Manasseh was captured and later released but we may conjecture that some Jews accompanied him into exile (II Chron. 33:11). Then came the various visits of Nebuchadnezzar (II Kings 24:1, 2; 24:10-16; 25:1-21; Jer. 52:31), which led to the exile of other groups of Jews. It would be impossible today to estimate the total number of people of general Israelite stock that eventually reached Mesopotamia.

But other lands such as Egypt[1] had their complement of exiles from Palestine. One wonders whether Pharaoh Shishak just before 900 B.C. took any captives to Egypt (I Kings 14:25). Certainly Pharaoh Necho, just before 600 B.C., took King Jehoahaz to Egypt (II Kings 23:34), and we may believe that he took also some of his subjects. It is not unlikely that after Nebuchadnezzar's first visit to Jerusalem in 598 B.C. Pharaoh

---

1. E. G. Kraeling, *The Brooklyn Museum Aramaic Papyri* (Yale, 1953), pp. 41-48, discusses the origin of the Jewish colony at Elephantine.

Hophra gave encouragement to Jews to rebel against the Chaldeans. An inscription of one Nesuhor, a prince under Hophra, tells of Syrians, Greeks, and Asiatics at Elephantine, and it is possible that there were Jews among these also. A further group of Jews, among whom was the prophet Jeremiah (Jer. 41-44), reached Egypt after the fall of Jerusalem in 586 B.C., although, unlike the exiles to Babylon, these came voluntarily and settled in the Delta area (Jer. 43:7). An interesting message is recorded in Jeremiah 44 in which the prophet addressed remarks to all the Jews in Egypt, both to those at Tahpanhes, Noph, and Migdol, all of which are in the northern part of the land, and also to those in the country of Patros, the region of southern or Upper Egypt. From this it would appear that at the time of Jeremiah there were Jews in both northern and southern Egypt.

Without doubt the people of Palestine were to be found in other areas, too, in the post-exilic period, and we shall not be surprised if future research reveals this to be so. Against the background of exile and dispersion of the people of Palestine, we can understand why it is that modern archaeologists have discovered important evidence of Jewish colonies in both Babylonia and Egypt during the present century.

THE DEVELOPMENT OF ARAMAIC AS AN INTERNATIONAL LANGUAGE

It will be wise before we discuss the Jewish colonies of Egypt and Babylonia to give some brief review of the way in which the Aramaic language came into prominence until it eventually became the medium of international correspondence in Persian times.[2] A group of people that may be regarded as one of the less important groups in the East, and which never rose as a people to the status of an empire, nevertheless gave to the great conquerors of their day a language and a script which provided them with the means of communication with their vast empire.

2. A. Dupont Somer, *Les Araméens* (Paris, 1949), gives a good outline, Chap. 6.

The Arameans are known from early times, possibly as early as 2000 B.C., when there is evidence of them in southern Mesopotamia.[3] The Assyrian inscriptions refer to them in 1320 B.C., and after the tenth century B.C. there is an abundance of written material in Aramaic. Certainly in the ninth, eighth, and seventh centuries B.C., and from then onwards, there is a good range of material from diverse regions in the general area represented today by Syria. This indicates that it was possible to write standard Aramaic from the first half of the ninth century B.C. We may say that before the little Aramean states were finally destroyed by the Assyrians, their language had attained such maturity that not only did it survive, but it was actually able to impose itself on the conquerors. From the ninth and eighth centuries onwards the Assyrian scribes needed to know Aramaic because of their dealings with the Arameans. The Bible in II Kings 18:26 makes reference to the fact that the Jewish leaders in Jerusalem invited the Assyrians to speak to them in Aramaic:

> Speak, I pray thee, to thy servants in the Syrian language [Aramaic]; for we understand it.

That Aramaic was known in Assyria is shown by a long letter written on a piece of pottery (an ostracon) in the days of Ashurbanipal, about 650 B.C. There are in addition standard weights in the shape of a lion from the ancient site of Nimrud marked with the names of Shalmaneser V, Sargon, and Sennacherib, and bearing some marks in Aramaic. At Nineveh the excavations brought to light numerous contracts dating from the seventh century B.C., written in the laborious cuneiform script, but carrying also a short summary in Aramaic to facilitate classification.

Two reasons for this widespread use of Aramaic may be suggested. It was a language that had a simple alphabet in contrast to the syllabic cuneiform (wedge-shaped) script of the Assyrians and others. It was also the language of the virile

---

3. A. Dupont Somer, "Sur les Débuts de l'histoire Araméenne," *Congress Volume* (Copenhagen, 1953), pp. 40f.

Arameans, thousands of whom had been taken captive through the centuries. Men of business began to use the script and the language, and once this step had been taken, progress was rapid.

Throughout the seventh century B.C., long Aramaic inscriptions were made in Syria proper. When the Chaldeans took over after the Assyrians they, too, knew Aramaic, as we know from numerous cuneiform tablets from the days of Nebuchadnezzar and Nabonidus, which carry notes in the Aramaic script, although the bulk of the tablet is written in cuneiform. There was clearly a complex linguistic situation in which Aramaic took its place alongside Akkadian.

A most interesting document from Egypt,[4] dating to the early years of the sixth century B.C., perhaps about 586, is written in Aramaic and is addressed to the Pharaoh by a Phoenician king named Adon who asks for help against the king of Babylon. Evidently the Phoenician prince believed that the Egyptian scribes could read Aramaic.

When Cyrus took over Babylon in 539 B.C. and the whole Chaldean Empire fell, Aramaic became the official language of Persian diplomacy. Under Darius I the empire spread from India to Egypt, and in order to keep in touch with this vast area Aramaic was used as the one language that would facilitate international contacts. It will suffice to state here that Aramaic documents from Persian times are known in abundance and have been found in almost all the provinces of the great empire from Egypt to India.[5]

A note of caution may be added just here. We have good evidence that the Persians used local languages at times along with Aramaic.[6] In Asia Minor there are inscriptions in Greek, including two stelae on the Bosporus, one in Greek and one

---

4. H. L. Ginsberg, "An Aramaic contemporary of the Lachish Letters," *Bulletin of the American Schools of Oriental Research*, No. 111, pp. 24f.

5. These are listed in A. Dupont Somer, *Les Araméens*, pp. 79-102.

6. A. T. Olmstead, *History of the Persian Empire* (Chicago, 1948), pp. 116, 297. Also R. P. R. de Vaux, "Les Décrets de Cyrus et de Darius," *Revue Biblique*, Jan. 1937, pp. 38-41.

in cuneiform, which Herodotus says were erected by Darius. In Egypt a set of laws was drawn up in demotic, the script of the common people, and correspondence between a satrap and the priests of Khnum was in demotic also. So it seems that there was flexibility in practice.

According to Esther 1:22, 3:12, and 8:9, Xerxes issued edicts to each of the people in its own tongue. Although this was evidently done at times, nevertheless the tremendous importance of Aramaic cannot be overlooked. We shall see in this chapter that the Jewish colony at Elephantine in southern Egypt used Aramaic a great deal during the fifth century B. C.

THE JEWISH COLONY AT NIPPUR IN BABYLONIA

In 1889 an American excavation conducted by the University of Pennsylvania began excavations in the ancient site of Nippur, to the south of old Babylon.[7] In the northwest area of the ruins the excavators discovered a remarkable collection of baked clay tablets in a room about 18 feet by 9 feet. There were some 730 tablets in this room comparable in quality of writing and appearance with those found in the library of the great Assyrian ruler Ashurbani-pal. These tablets were dated to the reigns of Artaxerxes I (465-424 B. C.) and Darius II (423-404 B.C.), but there was one tablet also from the reign of Artaxerxes II. The cache turned out to be the archives of a family of Babylonian businessmen, the Murashu family.

At the time of the discovery, tablets from this period were rare, and the find created a good deal of excitement, because it gave a remarkable insight into the business methods of those years. For the most part the tablets are plain commercial documents, contracts, receipts, lists of witnesses, letters, and the like. Much of the business was concerned with matters of agriculture, lands, crops, workmen, canals, public works, cattle, tools, vines, and trees. Payment was made by weighing out silver or occasionally gold.

The Murashu family ran a sort of banking business for ex-

7. See above p. 12.

change of moneys, and for payments[8] at a time when a new system of taxation had come into force in Persian lands. Introduced by Xerxes, its full rigor was experienced under Artaxeres I. In many areas in Mesopotamia, agricultural lands were held by what was called "bow" tenure, that is, the owners were obliged to furnish a bowman for the armed forces. This was an ancient custom, and as the years went by it became possible to commute the service to a money payment. With the rise of a new class of Persian officials, much of the land passed into the hands of the Persians by a clever trick. The former holders of "bow" lands, no longer required to send a bowman to the army, but required now to pay a money equivalent, often had to borrow money at 40 per cent per annum from such profiteers as the Murashu family. Their pledged lands were then worked by those rogues for their own advantage, until the title was completely lost to the original owners. When additional fields fell into the hands of the state because owners were unable to pay the taxes, there were corrupt officials who leased these lands to the same dishonest money lenders. We have already referred to the passage in the book of Nehemiah where some of the people complained that they were unable to help in the building of the walls because of the claims upon them for money, and the necessity for them to devote all their time to working their fields.

> We, our sons, and our daughters, are many; therefore we take up corn for them, that we may eat, and live. Some also there were that said, We have mortgaged our lands, vineyards, and houses, that we might buy corn, because of the dearth. There were also that said, We have borrowed money for the king's tribute, and that upon our lands and vineyards (Neh. 5:2-4).

In the troubled days following the death of Artaxerxes I the Murashu family needed to gain the goodwill of the new king whoever that might be. When finally Darius II emerged supreme, Enlil-nadinshum, the head of the firm, made a trip to greet his new master and to see that the privileged position

8. A. T. Olmstead, op. cit., pp. 299, 356, passim.

of the Murashu family was maintained. He evidently succeeded. Documents show that in the years that followed the Murashu sons acquired "bow" lands on an unprecedented scale. It would seem, however, that at last the authorities caught up with the rogues and after 417 B.C. the firm suddenly disappeared. It has been suggested that the royal commissioners finally ran the villains to earth, recovered the crown lands and punished the wrong-doers.

We have given this detail in order to underline some of the problems that confronted the people under the Persian administration, and to stress the way in which the small farmers were exploited by unscrupulous officials and bankers.

But there is another point about the archives of the Murashu bankers. These bankers recorded a great variety of names in their receipts and contracts. It is clear that they did business with many different peoples, Persians, Medes, Chaldeans, Arameans, and what is of special interest to us, Jews who seem to have been free citizens by then. There is a considerable number of Jewish names in the documents, pointing to the fact that numbers of the exiles did not return to Palestine but remained in the land, following the advice of Jeremiah (Jer. 29:1-7), to build houses and to seek the welfare of the city to which they had been exiled. Many of the names have the element *YAH* in them, like Yahulamu, Dadiya, Hananiah, Gedaliah and Pedaiah. Other well-known Jewish names occur, like Gadalyama, Ahiyama, Haggai, Benjamin, Natunu, Shabbata, and Mordecai. Over sixty Jewish names are known from the days of Artaxerxes, and over forty from the time of Darius II. It is of some interest to discover that the name Mordecai was especially common in the days of Artaxerxes I. It was, of course, in the time of his predecessor Xerxes, that the Bible places the story of Esther and the Jew Mordecai.

LIFE IN "YEB [ELEPHANTINE], THE FORTRESS"

There was a contrast between this settlement at Nippur in Babylonia and that at Elephantine in Egypt. The Nippur residents were part of a community that was engaged largely in agriculture and commerce, whereas the Elephantine colony had no agricultural pursuits to speak of, their means of livelihood being trade, shipping, stone quarrying, guarding the border, and attending to the taxes on goods that passed through this frontier post. In other words, the Elephantine colony was a military and administrative post.

The Aramaic texts of Elephantine speak of "Yeb the Fortress," and of "Syene the Fortress." Yeb was situated on a narrow island in the Nile, opposite modern Assuan, and Syene was on the site of Assuan itself. Syene was regarded as the southern limit of Egypt, and the phrase "from Migdol to Syene" is one that is known in the Bible (Ezek. 29:10, 30:6). In 1893 Charles Wilbour, an American traveler, acquired some valuable Aramaic papyri while visiting Assuan. A few years later, in 1904, Lady Cecil and Sir Robert Mond, two English visitors, bought some more, while yet others fell into the hands of German scholars. By 1914 a good number of these had been published and the world was given a remarkable glimpse into the life of a Jewish colony on this island in the Nile in the period 500 to 400 B.C. The documents were written in Aramic on papyri which, thanks to the dry land of Egypt, had been preserved all these years. They consisted of deeds, contracts, and letters, both private and official. The translation of these documents enabled the scholars to form an idea of how the affairs of daily life were conducted and by what laws the people of this colony were governed.[9]

All transactions were safeguarded by agreements, and contracts were drawn up in proper manner, attested by witnesses, and then rolled up and sealed. Finally, a note was added to the outside of the document to identify it. The procedure is not very different from that followed by Jeremiah in the purchase of his field (Jer. 32:8ff.), and is basically the Babylonian method which was adopted by the Persians. Most of

9. Discussions and translations are available in J. B. Pritchard, *Ancient Near Eastern Texts* (Princeton, 1950), pp. 222-223, 491ff., E. G. Kraeling, *op. cit.*, and A Cowley, *Aramaic Papyri of the Fifth Century B. C.* (Oxford, 1923).

the documents at Elephantine carry two dates, one in Egyptian style and one in Babylonian style, so that we have no doubt about the date at which they were written.

Marriage contracts, as we might expect, are numerous and show that marriages were generally arranged between the bridegroom and someone acting for the bride. It was usual for the groom to give a bridal gift. In case of divorce (which seems to have been rare, to judge from the few documents referring to it), the husband lost his marriage gift. It was possible for the wife also to sue for divorce. One woman whose name was Mibtahiah was involved in more than one marriage.

Slavery was known in Yeb and slaves were bought and sold, or perhaps inherited. One poor female slave, with three sons, had her children divided on the death of her master. There is, on the other hand, a case where a slave was freed and seems to have become the heir of his master.

Many of the documents deal with loaning and borrowing, and it is evident that both men and women were able to engage in business. The interest rate on loans was high, as much as 60 percent in some instances, with the threat that if the sum were not repaid, the interest would be added to the capital, and the same rate of interest charged. Modern wives will find interest in the case of a husband who used his wife's money and had to write out a promissory note to repay within a month. To the lady's credit it should be added that she charged no interest. Other business contracts deal with all manner of things. One case is recorded where two men signed a receipt for a load of barley they received from a boatman, and promised to deliver it to a certain company of soldiers.

Real estate transactions were common. The Jews could buy and sell houses and make legal transfer of gifts of houses and lands. Daughters seem to have been specially favored as the recipients of houses, and more particularly on the occasion of marriage.

Litigation was common in Elephantine for all kinds of reasons. It is clear that Jews could go to law in civil matters, and the case would be heard before the Persian-Egyptian courts, although in internal matters affecting the Jewish community the matter was dealt with by the priests. Typical civil cases were disputes about land, boundaries, possession of stock, and stealing.

There was regular correspondence sent and received by the people in the colony. Letters generally began with salutations to the temple of the deity, followed by the name of the addressee, the name of the writer, and the wish that God may permit seeing the face of the addressee in peace. After all these formalities came the formal requests, some of which are very modern. One man asks a friend to visit him; another complains that since his friend came to live in Syene he had not seen him; yet another sends greetings from several friends. So the simple matters of the common life are discussed. Generally the letters were written on papyrus, but some were written on broken pieces of pottery (ostraca).

Among the most interesting of the papyri are several that consist of little more than lists of people. One contains the names of those who contributed gifts to the temple at Yeb. There are 123 names on the list, many of them being women, and it may be regarded as a sort of "Who's Who" in the colony of Yeb. The correspondence relating to government affairs, and especially the important letter addressed to the governor of Judah, requires a special discussion.

Glimpses into the Persian government that was in existence in Egypt at the time are also to be gained from these papyri.[10] Thus the satrap at the time of Xerxes was Achaemenes. His successor, who features a good deal in the documents and who functioned under both Artaxerxes I and Darius II, was Arsham (Greek, Arsames). In matters of government there were various departments, each of which had a presiding individual assisted by a group of colleagues. At the head of the chancery from which the orders of Arsham were issued, was a chancellor, who is called in Aramaic, *be'el te'em,* which is precisely

10. E. G. Kraeling, *op. cit.,* pp. 27-40.

the name found in the Bible in Ezra 4:9 for Rehum, who is there associated with a number of other officials, "the scribe and the rest of the companions." It was this group that took action as a body against the builders of the wall of Jerusalem early in the reign of Artaxerxes I. It is of interest also to learn that at Elephantine there was another Rehum, who occupied much the same sort of post. In the provinces, the head man was a *pekid* or "officer," a title known both in Persian contexts and in the Bible (Esther 2:3, Neh. 11:9, etc.) [11] and which had a variety of connotations. It is clear that the Persians in Egypt used peoples of various nationalities in this and similar posts. In the letter addressed to the governor of Judah, the term is *peha,* which is also a Biblical word. Other Persian titles that appear either here at Elephantine, or elsewhere, occur in the Bible. One common Persian title for "treasurers," *gizbarayya,* does not happen to occur in the Elephantine texts, but it is found in the Bible in Ezra 7:21. The list in Ezra 4:9, which commences with Rehum and goes on to speak of the *Dinaites,* is really referring to the "judges." The Aramaic texts before us throw a great deal of light on the function of these "judges" in a typical Persian colony. All of these insights into Persian methods of administration add at the same time to our understanding of the Biblical records, for time and again we discover that the Bible has used a title that has a specific Persian connotation.

THE RELIGION OF THE JEWISH COLONY

The Jews in Egypt still worshipped Yahweh, the God of Israel. They built a temple for worship on the island of Yeb, and contributed to its upkeep. They observed the feast of unleavened bread, for we learn from a document dated in 419 B.C. that Darius the king had sent to Arsham the satrap a letter, ordering the Egyptian Jews to celebrate the feast from the 15th to the 21st of Nisan. While there is no reference to the Pass-

11. Hebrew, *Pakid*, used in Gen. 41:34, Jer. 20:1, II Chron. 24:11, Judg. 9:28, etc.

over as such, it is likely that the Jews observed this also. There
are one or two texts that show that the Sabbath was observed
also. For example, one sentence on an ostracon reads

Tie up the ass tomorrow on the sabbath lest he stray.

It is not certain that the Jews of Elephantine had copies of
the Jewish scriptures with them. There are some sentences in
the papyri that suggest that they had parts of Deuteronomy,
and perhaps of Genesis, but this is not beyond doubt.[12] The
only literary piece that we know for certain that they pos-
sessed was the story of Ahikar, an ancient worthy who had
various exciting adventures and acquired a good deal of sound
wisdom which he passed on to his son. The story comprised a
piece of wisdom literature rather like some of the literature
of the Bible and the sacred books of other peoples.[13]

We cannot, of course, argue from silence and conclude that
the Jews here had no Biblical literature simply because no
pieces of the Bible have been found. It may be one of the
accidents of preservation that it is chiefly documents of a business character that have been found.

It is to be further noted that in the temple of Yahu (Yahweh) sacrifices were offered. Reference will be made below to
the letter addressed to the governor of Judah in which it is
pointed out that when this temple at Yeb was destroyed, it was
no longer possible to offer meal offerings, incense, or burnt
offerings. Two priests are mentioned, as well as a servant of
Yahu, indicating that there was evidently a well-organized
ritual in use at the temple of Elephantine.

One disconcerting feature of the Jewish religion at Yeb is
the fact that evidently some kind of syncretism was tolerated.
The long list of contributors to the temple of Yahu indicates
that of the total sum collected, certain moneys were earmarked
for Eshem-bethel and 'Anat-bethel. The distribution was,
Yahu, 246 shekels, Eshem-bethel, 140 shekels, and 'Anat-bethel

12. E. G. Kraeling, *op. cit.*, pp. 97-99.
13. J. B. Pritchard, *op. cit.*, pp. 427-430.

240 shekels.[14]   The element Bethel in the latter two names
frequently occurs as the name of a god from the seventh to the
fourth century B.C. in Canaanite-Aramean contexts.   A third
name that has a divine connotation, *Herem,* is found on other
documents from Elephantine.   The conclusion of W. F. Albright, whose discussion we have followed here, is as follows:[15]

> There can, accordingly, be no reasonable doubt that we are
> confronted with Aramaic syncretism, arising about the seventh
> century B. C. in Jewish circles which were under strong pagan
> influence.

In another place the same writer discusses the possibility
that these names may represent substitutes for the name of
God:[16]

> The three divine names Eshem-bethel, Herem-bethel, Anat-
> bethel (Anat-Yahu), meaning respectively, "Name of the house
> of God" (God), "Sacredness of the house of God," and "Sign
> (?) of the house of God" would reflect pure hypostatizations of
> deity . . . .

Possibly the same happened here as in later Judaism, where
a fence was built around the holiness of God by substituting
words denoting aspects or qualities of God, such as Divine Wisdom, or the Divine Word, or the Divine Presence, for the name
of God. There remains, however, something of uncertainty about
the exact nature of the religion in Elephantine. We naturally
think of the picture of the religion of the Jews in the years just
before and just after the exile in Judah itself. Indeed, at various times syncretism was very serious in both Judah and Israel and was strongly assailed by more than one prophet. If
that happened in the homeland, there is no reason why it
should not have happened in a foreign land like Egypt.

Such divergences from the official orthodox view of the
priests in Jerusalem would not be tolerated by them for a moment, and it was unthinkable that there should be a second

14. W. F. Albright, *Archaeology and the Religion of Israel*
(Baltimore, 1956), p. 169.
15. *Ibid.,* p. 171.
16. W. F. Albright, *From Stone Age to Christianity* (New York,
1957), p. 373.

temple beside the one in Jerusalem. This comes out clearly in the letter which we now take up for discussion.

LETTER TO THE GOVERNOR OF JUDAH FROM THE PEOPLE OF YEB

One of the most striking of the letters found among the Aramaic documents at Yeb was one dated in 407 B.C. It was a petition to the governor of Judah to assist in the rebuilding of the temple in Yeb. The circumstances seem to be these.[17] At some earlier time, even before the days of Cambyses, the Jews had built a temple in Elephantine.

> Our forefathers built this temple in the fortress of Elephantine, back in the days of the kingdom of Egypt, and when Cambyses came to Egypt he found it built. They knocked down all the temples of the gods of Egypt but no one did any damage to this temple.

When Darius II came to the throne after violent measures, his brother rose against him and there were uprisings in many of the provinces, such as Asia Minor, Media, and Egypt, in the years 410 to 408 B.C. It is possible to deduce from the documents available that, whereas the Jews were formerly in the service of the Egyptians and served them loyally, they were now in the service of the Persians and served them loyally too. In the troubles of these years, when the satrap Arsham was recalled for consultation with Darius II at the start of his reign, the local Egyptians took the opportunity to attack the Jews. There was conspiracy with the local officials, Widrang (Vidarang), the local Persian chief, and his son cooperating with the Egyptians, probably for personal gain.[18]

> In the month of Tammuz, in the 14th year of King Darius, when Arsames departed and went to the King, the priests of the god Khnub, who is in the fortress of Elephantine, conspired with Vidarang, who was commander in chief here, to wipe out the temple of the god Yaho from the fortress of Elephantine. So that wretch Vidarang sent to his son Nefeyan who was in command of the garrison of the fortress of Syene this order:

17. J. B. Pritchard, *op. cit.*, p. 492, col. 1.
18. *Ibid.*, col. 1.

"The temple of the god Yaho in the fortress of Yeb is to be destroyed.

The temple was duly razed, its pillars of stone, its five gateways, and its roof of cedarwork were destroyed and fire set to the ruins. The basins of gold and silver and other articles in the temple were taken off. Subsequently, after a long period of fasting and praying to Yaho, the god of heaven had allowed them to have some cause of rejoicing over their enemy, for the Persians had duly punished him and demoted him.

The next part of the story concerns the letter which was written by the Jews of Elephantine to the priests in Jerusalem, which, though not in existence, is referred to in the letter to the governor. There was no answer to this, so the people wrote to the governor himself, and this is the letter we now have. Its main purpose is to ask the governor Bagoas (Bigvai) to give some help in the rebuilding of the temple in Elephantine since the Egyptians "do not allow us to build."[19]

> Your servants Yedoniah, and his colleagues, and the Jews, the citizens of Elephantine, all thus say: If it please our lord, take thought of this temple to rebuild it, since they do not let us rebuild it. Look to your well-wishers and friends here in Egypt. Let a letter be sent from you to them concerning the temple of the god Yaho to build it in the fortress of Elephantine as it was built before.

If Bagoas would do this they offered to pray for him, and to offer meal offerings and incense and sacrifice to Yaho. They assured him that merit would be stored up before Yaho by this act, greater than the merit of those who sacrificed the value of one thousand talents.

Two other important facts are given in the letter. First, these Jews of Elephantine stated that they had written to the high priest in Jerusalem, Johanan and his colleagues the priests, and to Ostanes (Ustan), the brother of Asani and the nobles of the Jews. To this letter there had been no reply. Secondly, they stated that they had written to Delaiah and Shelemiah, the sons of Sanballat the governor of Samaria.

19. *Ibid.*, col. 2.

These two facts are most significant, for they give us a glimpse into Judah and Palestine at the close of the fifth century B.C. We learn that Bagoas was governor, Johanan was high priest, and Sanballat was still alive, although his two sons were of some importance, owing no doubt to the age of their father. It was useless for the people of Elephantine to ask further help from the religious leaders at Jerusalem for that door was evidently closed. It has been argued by some scholars that the Jerusalem priests regarded the Jews in Egypt as semi-heretical, and therefore did not encourage them in their apostasy.[20] If that was so, the only hope of help for the Jews at Yeb was to work through the Persian political leaders, Bagoses and Sanballat.

The outcome of this letter is full of interest. Request was made that Bagoas should write to the Jews in Egypt and inform them of his plans to help. What happened was that the emissary brought back some verbal information.[21]

Memorandum of what Bagohi and Delaiah said to me. Memorandum. Let it be an instruction to you to say in Egypt before Arsham concerning the altar house of the god of heaven which in Yeb the fortress was built formerly before Cambyses, which Widrang, the evildoer did cast down in the year 14 of Darius the king, that it should be rebuilt in its place, as it was formerly, and that meal offerings and frankincense should be brought upon that altar corresponding to what formerly was done.

It is not clear just how the Jewish colony in Egypt stood under the protection of the governor of Judah, but he agreed that they should go to Arsames and report these facts. It is interesting to note that the new temple was to be a place where the only offerings were to be the non-blood offerings. This has led some writers to suggest that the governor of Judah may have consulted the priests in Jerusalem, as well as the nobles, before giving his opinion. In the end it seems that the temple in Elephantine was finally rebuilt. One document dated to

20. Logically, of course, other answers may be given. The writer assumes that the worship in Jerusalem, despite certain defects, was essentially true to the divine intention in that age.

21. E. G. Kraeling, op. cit., p. 106.

402 B.C., in referring to a certain house that changed owner-ship, located it on the west of the temple of Yaho, which sug-gests that the temple and the cult were still in existence then.

This is the last we hear of the Jewish colony. Persian con-trol in Egypt ceased just at the turn of the century.[22] The Jewish colony "which burst mysteriously into the historical pic-ture with the coming of Cambyses, disappears from it equally mysteriously a few years after the eclipse of Persian rule."[23]

THE DATE OF NEHEMIAH

The material in the papyri from Elephantine enables us to date Nehemiah very firmly in the reign of Artaxerxes I. The high priest referred to in the papyri is Johanan, who, accord-ing to Nehemiah 12:22, was the second high priest after Eliashib, the priest referred to in the days of Nehemiah. Again in Nehemiah 12:10-11 we have a list which places Johanan (or Jonathan) after Eliashib. Another significant reference is to be found in Josephus,[24] who speaks of an officer of the Persians, Bagoses, and a high priest named John (Johanan). Accord-ing to this reference, Bagoses, living in the days of Johanan, must have ruled after Nehemiah. Bagoses is the governor re-ferred to in the Aramaic letter we have just considered for the year 407 B.C. Evidently, the Sanballat referred to is the same man as we meet in the days of Nehemiah, but now grown older. We are led to the conclusion that Nehemiah lived be-fore 407 B.C. Since he went to Jerusalem in the twentieth year of King Artaxerxes, we look for a king of this name who ruled prior to 407 B.C. This is, of course, Artaxerxes I, who reigned from 465 to 425 B.C., which means that Nehemiah's arrival in Jerusalem is to be dated in 444 B.C. In a most exciting way, the discovery of some Aramaic papyri in Egypt, hundreds of miles away from Palestine, enables us to give an exact date to an important Bible character.

22. *Ibid.*, Chapter 10, pp. 111-119.
23. *Ibid.*, p. 115.
24. Josephus, *Antiquities*, Book XI, vii. 1.

After the close of the fifth century B.C. we enter upon a period of great obscurity for the Jews. Yet there were important things happening all around them which had a vital bearing on their future history. Thanks to archaeological research we can pierce the darkness just a little.

CHAPTER FIVE

THE COMING OF THE GREEKS

―――――――

THE FOURTH CENTURY B.C. was to witness the collapse of
Persian power in the East and the rise of the Greeks. At the
close of the fifth century the Persian ruler was Artaxerxes II
(404-361 B.C.), whose reign was not without merit, although
he lost control in Egypt following the revolt of his brother
Cyrus. The famous Greek expedition in which the Greek
writer Xenophon took part contributed to the Persian loss of
Egypt. Thirty years after the death of Artaxerxes II the great
Persian Empire collapsed. But before the final collapse Artaxerxes III (Ochus), a brutal man, had a measure of success and was able to restore some of the lost fortunes of the
Persians. He recovered Egypt in 342 B.C. and was able to
quell revolts in the general area of Phoenicia. There are
hints in some ancient records that the Jews were involved in
these revolts and that some of them were exiled to the area
of the Caspian Sea.[1] The last Persian king, Darius III, was
faced with the impossible task of opposing the might of Alexander the Great. By 331 B.C. the Persians were no more and
the East fell into the hands of the Greeks. In this chapter we
shall follow the fortunes of the Jews in Palestine for the period 331 B.C. to 63 B.C., during which Greek rulers controlled
the land, and at the end of which Palestine fell into the hands
of the Romans.

1. For example, the Chronicle of Eusebius.

Nabataean temple at Petra (see p. 83).

Matson Photo Service

Corniced tomb at Petra, with Nabataean inscription (see p. 83).

Matson Photo Service

Matson   Photo   Serv-

Above: Ruins of Herod's Towers at the West Gate of Samaria (see p. 129(see p. 129

Below: Jewish Wailing Wall, showing the Herodian masonry (see p. 126(see p. 126
Courtesy of Oriental Institute, University of Chica-

BRIEF HISTORICAL OUTLINE, 331 B.C. TO 63 B.C.

Alexander the Great, son of Philip of Macedon, was born in the year 356 B.C. At the age of twenty he came to the throne of Macedon on the assassination of his father. The various states around Macedonia seemed to think that the treaties with Philip ended on his death, but they were to learn that the young Alexander was as strong as his father. Very soon he subdued all these and decided on an invasion of Persia. By 331 B.C. he was master of the East. Yet his life was to ebb away in June 323 B.C. before he was thirty-three years old. Almost at once his empire was divided between his generals. The senior general Perdiccas tried to hold the empire together and the various generals were assigned to satrapies. We are especially interested in Ptolemy, who went to Egypt, and Seleucus, who went to Babylon. But the scheme did not work and before long war broke out. There was fighting for several years, but by 315 B.C. four leaders had emerged. Ptolemy Lagi ruled in Egypt, the most compact of the four kingdoms, where he was assisted by General Seleucus, who had been forced out of Babylon by the second leader, Antigonus, who ruled in Syria and central Asia. Then Cassander held Macedonia, and Lysimachus held Thrace. When Antigonus tried to exert greater claims in the Palestine area, he came into conflict with Ptolemy and Seleucus, and in 312 B.C. these two defeated him at Gaza and obtained control of Palestine and parts of Syria. Seleucus seized this moment to dash across the desert to Babylon and to reinstate himself in his old satrapy. This was the commencement of the Seleucid dynasty. Eleven years later Antigonus was again defeated and Seleucus extended his boundaries to the north and established his capital at Antioch. The final outcome of all this strife, as far as Palestine was concerned, was that from now on the Ptolemies and the Seleucids were to strive for the possession of the Holy Land. For the first hundred years till 198 B.C., Palestine was ruled by the Ptolemies, but after this it passed into the hands of the Seleucids and remained, nominally at least, a Seleucid possession till the Romans took over the land in 63 B.C.

We can distinguish three periods in the Seleucid rule: (1) from 198 B.C. till 175 B.C., a period of undisputed Seleucid rule, (2) from 175 B.C. till 135 B.C., the period of the Maccabean struggle, and (3) from 135 B.C. till 63 B.C., the period of nominal Seleucid rule during which there was a great deal of real independence for the Jews. With the coming of the Romans in 63 B.C. Jewish independence was finally lost.

We have some valuable archaeological evidence for the years 400 B.C. to about 50 B.C., and even if it is not great in quantity it does help to fill out the written records.[2] The latter part of the period is better supplied with such evidence than the earlier.

EDOMITES, IDUMEANS, AND NABATAEANS

During the three centuries under consideration, the history of the Jews, though incomplete in many places, touches again and again on the old Edomites, now known as Idumeans, and a newer group called Nabataeans. Archaeological work in Transjordan has given some additional information about the Edomites during these years. It will be remembered that at the time of the fall of Judah in 586 B.C. these people exploited the situation in southern Judah and invaded the area. They were to be overwhelmed in their own homeland by other Arab groups before the end of the fifth century. Excavations at the old port of Ezion Geber, which was originally founded by Solomon, have produced seal impressions from City IV which contain names that are clearly Edomite.[3] But by the fifth century ostraca carry names that are Arab in character.[4] We may conclude that with the rise of the Arabs belonging to the group that produced the Geshem of Nehemiah's day, the Edomites quite lost their power. Many moved to Judah, while

2. W. F. Albright, *Archaeology of Palestine* (London, 1956), p. 147.

3. Nelson Glueck, "The Topography and History of Ezion Geber and Elath," *Bulletin of the American Schools of Oriental Research*, No. 72, pp. 11-12.

4. Nelson Glueck, "Ostraca from Elath," *Bulletin of the American Schools of Oriental Research*, No. 80, pp. 3-10.

others were absorbed. In southern Judah they lived on and
became known as the Idumeans. We have valuable evidence
about them here from some tombs found at Marisa which
date to the middle of the third century B.C. These will be
described in some detail later.[5] A variety of inscriptions, containing many names, indicates that Edomites lived alongside
other types of people like Phoenician settlers. The names are
recorded in Greek for the most part, but there are some in
Aramaic, among which there are those with the divine element
Qos, the name of the chief god of old Edom. Interestingly
enough, Josephus refers to the husband of Salome, the sister
of Herod, as "Kostobaros, an Idumean by birth . . . whose
ancestors had been priests of Koze, whom the Idumeans had
formerly worshipped as a god."[6]

In due course the Arab group that replaced the Edomites
was itself repaced by the Nabataeans, who appear first in recorded history in 312 B.C., when Antigonus the Greek decided
to attack them.[7] His general actually took the high rock behind Petra, the refuge of the ancient Edomites, but success was
shortlived because the troops were wiped out as they were returning home. The researches of Nelson Glueck have shown
that the land of Edom had no serious sedentary occupation
during the whole Persian period.[8] Then came the Nabataeans,
who gave up their own Arabic tongue for Aramaic, as thousands of inscriptions show today, and slowly settled down to
build towns and to live an urban life. Petra became their great
center, and here they undertook the remarkable task of carv-
ing out homes and temples in the red sandstone of the valley.
There is a good deal of inaccurate talk in some circles where,
in order to show how the prophecies that foretold the downfall and desolation of Edom at last came true, pictures of

5. See below, pp. 86, 87.
6. Josephus, *Antiquities*, XV, vii, 9.
7. Jean Starcky, "The Nabataeans — A Historical Sketch," *Biblical Archaeologist*, Dec. 1955.
8. Nelson Glueck, Reports in *Annual of the American Schools of
Oriental Research*, Vol. 15. Also, *The Other Side of Jordan* (New
Haven, 1940).

rock-cut dwellings and temples in Petra are shown as Edomite buildings. These structures are undoubtedly Nabataean. The only Edomite site in the area is on the hill behind Petra, where there is evidence of occupation in Edomite times.[9] Of special interest in the Nabataean areas are the High Places where these Nabataeans offered sacrifices to their gods. These may give some idea of the kind of thing referred to so often in the days of the great prophets of Israel. Quite a deal of excavation has gone on in Nabataean sites, so that today we know something of the coinage, the splendid pottery, the architecture, and the fortresses erected in strategic places to guard their frontiers. One of their kings, Aretas, is known in the New Testament in II Corinthians 11:32 as the king who controlled Damascus at the time Paul escaped over the wall in a basket.

At the period under discussion in this chapter, the Nabataeans were just coming into their own. They were to have dealings with the Greeks, the Maccabees, the Idumeans, and the Romans before they were finally overcome by the Romans just after 100 A.D.

ARCHAEOLOGICAL EVIDENCE FROM THE DAYS OF THE PTOLEMIES

There were five Ptolemies who controlled Palestine from Egypt in the third century B.C.; Ptolemy I, Soter (323-285 B.C.), Ptolemy II, Philadelphus (285-246 B.C.), Ptolemy III, Euergetes I, (246-221 B.C.), Ptolemy IV, Philopater (221-203 B.C.), and Ptolemy V, Epiphanes (203-180 B.C.). There was a good deal of conflict with the Seleucids during the century that the Ptolemies ruled, and Palestine again became a battlefield over which two empires fought. Under the first of these rulers many Jews were taken to Egypt and forced to live in Alexandria, where Greek soon became their language. Ptolemy II released many of them in view of troubles with the second and third Seleucid rulers, Antiochus I (280-262 B. C.),

9. W. H. Morton, "Umm el-Biyara," *Biblical Archaeologist*, May, 1956, pp. 26f.

and Antiochus II (261-247 B.C.). Finally a treaty was made and a marriage arranged between Antiochus II and the daughter of Ptolemy II. This soon failed when the daughter of the Egyptian was murdered, and soon after, his son Ptolemy III waged war on the Seleucid ruler. Further wars followed till finally the Seleucid king Antiochus III, the Great (223-187 B.C.), was able to overwhelm all Egyptian resistance and enter Judah as ruler in 198 B.C. The story is told in a peculiarly disguised fashion in Daniel, Chapter 11.

Points of archaeological interest during these years may now be mentioned. We have referred already to the important papyri discovered in Egypt from the archives of Zeno, an official in the government of Ptolemy II.[10] Tobiah, an Ammonite who sent gifts of animals to the Pharaoh, features among these documents, and as we have seen, the find gives valuable insight into the condition of Transjordan at the time. Another Egyptian papyrus dated to 259 B.C. refers to the purchase of a "Babylonian slave girl" of seven years in Birta of Ammantis, which is identical with the fortress of Tobias. The witnesses to this document are described as "clerechs of the cavalry of Tubias," that is, they were soldier settlers with plots of land. Evidently, then, Tobias had military forces at his disposal and guarded this part of Ptolemy's domains. Perhaps the position of this Tobias under Ptolemy of Egypt was similar to that occupied by his forefather, Tobiah the Ammonite, under Artaxerxes I, the Persian.[11]

Further evidence from Egypt concerns the presence of a considerable Jewish colony there at the time. Epigraphic evidence from the third century B.C., including two Jewish-Aramaic papyri, and at least eight ostraca from Edfu in Upper Egypt, and from the site known as Zawiyet el-Meitin, all point to the presence of Jews in the land. That there were Jews in the region of Alexandria is clear from the Zeno

10. See above, pp. 54, 55. See also, C. C. McCown, "The Araq el-Emir and the Tobiads," *Biblical Archaeologist*, Sept., 1957, pp. 63f.

11. C. C. McCown, *op. cit.*, p. 70.

papyri which contain Jewish names. To these may be added Aramaic tomb inscriptions from Alexandria, and Aramaic writing on coins from Demanhur, nearby. The personal names revealed are partly Biblical names, partly Aramaic, and partly Greek.[12]

It was during the years of Ptolemy II that, according to the story told on the spurious letter of Aristeas, the king called together Jewish scholars to translate the Torah into Greek for inclusion in the great library that he founded at Alexandria. The names of the men supposed to have been chosen are certainly in line with the names revealed in the epigraphic evidence we have already referred to. While we have none of the original manuscripts of this Septuagint translation into Greek, it is fairly clear that in the period 300 to 250 B.C. the Torah was translated.

One other important find from Egypt from these days is a small piece of papyrus containing the ten commandments in Hebrew, the so-called Nash papyrus.[13] Evidently some of the Jews in Egypt in the third century B.C. could still read Hebrew.

Some of the sites excavated in Palestine have produced coins of this period, and naturally there is an abundance of pottery to show that many sites were occupied. The one group of important monuments of the period is the painted tombs of Marisa in southwestern Judah, the Old Testament Mareshah, and the modern Tell Sandahannah. The tombs, discovered in 1902 by J. P. Peters and H. Thiersch, lay near to the tell which represented the most important town in the area. They were originally excavated from the soft limestone rock and painted inside in a most elaborate fashion. Free spaces on the walls were occupied by inscriptions and graffiti (drawings and writing scratched on the walls), in Greek and Aramaic. The personal names were Greek, Phoenician, and Edomite (Idumean). We are especially interested in the site

12. W. F. Albright, *From Stone Age to Christianity* (New York, 1957), p. 349.
13. *Ibid.*, pp. 345, 350.

because Ptolemy II established a Sidonian colony here under an official named Apollophanes, whose epitaph is preserved in one of the tombs. When the tombs were first opened the colors of the frescoes around the walls were quite bright, but they have now faded. One tomb had a long procession of animals, some of which were real, and others of which were imaginary. W. F. Albright has suggested that they may have been based on some book of illustrations of wild life sketched from the zoological gardens of Alexandria.[14] The predominance of Greek names on the walls may simply mean that the Phoenicians and the Idumeans who lived there were Hellenized by that time. One of the tombs had a remarkable painting of tall cressets for carrying torches or lamps. These were painted on opposite piers in the vestibule of one of the tombs, and may have represented incense stands, the like of which are known from pictures and from carvings on coins from the general area of Phoenicia. Albright sees in them a possible source of information about the two tall pillars that stood outside the temple of Solomon.[15] The worship of the region was evidently syncretistic, with elements of Edomite, Phoenician, and Greek religion. The town of Marisa was a well-planned town of Greek pattern, with streets at right angles forming blocks of houses.[16] There was a market place next to the gate, rectangular in shape, open at one end and with shops on three sides. The material from the tombs in the area combines to give the impression that this area was thoroughly Hellenized by the middle of the third century B.C. It was this Hellenization that was to lead to much of the Maccabean trouble in the second century, when the orthodox Jews resisted the changes.

14. W. F Albright, *Archaeology of Palestine* (London, 1956), p. 149.
15. W. F. Albright, *Archaeology and the Religion of Israel* (Baltimore, 1956), pp. 144-146; also, "Two cressets from Marisa and the pillars of Jachin and Boaz," *Bulletin of the American Schools of Oriental Research*, Feb., 1942, p. 18f.
16. W. F. Albright, *Archaeology of Palestine* (London, 1956), p. 153.

The town of Bethel at this time shows three phases of occupation between the fourth century and 70 A.D. The first phase covers the Ptolemaic and the Seleucid period down to the reign of Antiochus IV, and it presumably came to an end with the campaigns of General Bacchides about 160 B.C. The coins give the story, for there were ten Ptolemaic coins from the years 285 B.C. to 182 B.C. and four coins of Antiochus IV.

The town of Tell en Nasbeh, north of Jerusalem, produced coins of Ptolemy II, as well as coins of both earlier and later periods.

The important town of Shechem in central Palestine which played a prominent part in the earlier history of Israel was apparently unoccupied between the eighth and the fourth centuries B.C. But towards the end of the fourth century it was reoccupied. Coins of the first two Ptolemies bear witness to occupation in the period 312 to 246 B.C.[17]

ARCHAEOLOGICAL EVIDENCE FROM THE PERIOD 198 B.C. TO 134 B.C.

When Antiochus III entered Palestine in 198 B.C. there commenced an era of great trouble for the Jews which was aggravated by the fact that some of the Jews were sympathetic to the desire of the Greek rulers to introduce Greek culture all over the East. When Antiochus was defeated by the Romans in Asia Minor and was required to pay heavy indemnity to them, the Seleucid ruler sought ways and means to raise the money. This caused further conflicts with the Jews, for in the days of his successor, Seleucus IV (187-175 B.C.), efforts were made to seize the Temple funds in Jerusalem. There were those priests who aided and abetted the Seleucids in their scheme. Matters were made worse when the Seleucid rulers interfered with the Zadokite succession of the high priesthood. It was really in the days of Antiochus IV (175-163 B.C.) that

17. G. E. Wright, "The Second Campaign at Tell Balatah (Shechem)," *Bulletin of the American Schools of Oriental Research*, No. 148, December, 1957, p. 27.

matters came to a head. This man who had been taken as a hostage to Rome as a boy and had learned the ways of Rome, had learned also to fear the Romans. At the start of his reign he appointed a certain Jason as high priest in the place of the true high priest, Onias, because this man promised to raise more in taxation and to assist in the Hellenizing processes. Many Greek practices were introduced into Judah, and especially into the capital, Jerusalem. Pious men, who were known as the Hasidim, resisted these changes. Eventually the priest Jason was replaced by Menelaus, who offered to raise still more money for the foreign rulers. At a later stage, Antiochus decided to invade Egypt, and at first had some success, but when he went a second time, he was ordered out of Egypt by the Romans. One thing and another aggravated him, and finally he found an excuse to vent his spite on the Jews. He forbade them to read their scriptures and to practice their religion. Worst of all, he desecrated their Temple and offered pagan sacrifices there. The Jews rebelled under the family of the Hasmoneans, whom we now know as the Maccabees, a name given to one of their leaders and possibly derived from a Hebrew word meaning "hammerer." From 168 B.C. till 142 B.C. the Jewish patriots waged incessant war against their enemies, being led at first by the aged Mattathias, and then in turn by his three sons, Judas (166-160 B.C.), Jonathan (160-142 B.C.), and Simon (142-134 B.C.).

Judas was able to defeat a number of Seleucid armies, and by the end of 165 B.C. the Jews were allowed to return to the Temple and were granted religious freedom. But they wanted political liberty too, and the war went on. To strengthen the hand of the Jews, Judas built forts, one of the most interesting of which was the fort at Bethzur, to the south of Bethlehem. By 161 B.C. this was taken by the Seleucid general Bacchides, who destroyed it and rebuilt on the site to a Greek plan.

When Judas was slain in battle, Jonathan took his place. Before his death he was able to consolidate the position of the Jews greatly. He was actually appointed high priest by a usurper of the Seleucid throne to whom he gave support. This usurper, Balas by name, made many concessions, and when he died and a new king took control in Antioch, Jonathan besieged Jerusalem, which was in the hands of the Seleucids. The price of lifting the siege was a lightening of taxation and the granting of certain areas near Samaria to Jonathan. When further troubles in Antioch brought a change in Seleucid policy, Jonathan supported another rebel named Tryphon, and proceeded at once to Bethzur, the Seleucid fortress, and took it. But Tryphon was afraid of Jonathan and had him trapped and imprisoned. The leadership passed to his brother Simon. Before long Simon had captured Gezer, another Seleucid stronghold, and had taken the fortress in Jerusalem itself. The Jews were so pleased at these successes that they accepted Simon formally as high priest, even though he was not of the correct family. Simon also gained recognition by the Roman Senate of the day, but he met his death by treachery at the hands of his son-in-law. It was under Simon that the Jews emerged again into real independence. The family to which he belonged, the Hasmoneans, were now both the ruling family and the high-priestly family. Civil and religious authority were vested in them. This had its problems, but from 142 B.C. till 63 B.C. the Jews preserved their independence, even though the Seleucids at times endeavored to exert control over them. The Jews had an ambition to recover lands lost to their enemies, and the Seleucids made one or two abortive attempts to regain control of the Jews. But before we take up that story, we shall collect the archaeological material for the period 198 B.C. to 134 B.C.

Our information comes from the excavation of several important sites, among which Bethzur, Samaria, Marisa, and Gezer feature as especially valuable. We must remember that the Greek conquerors, in pursuance of their Hellenizing policy, built towns all over their domains. In Palestine several towns were repeopled and numbers of Greek colonists settled there. Thus Samaria was repeopled by colonists from Macedonia; and coastal towns like Gaza, Ascalon, Caesarea, Dor, and Ptolemais became Greek cities. East of Jordan there were numerous Hellenized towns, and in the mountain areas such places as Bethshan (Scythopolis) and Gezer became Greek cities in addition to Samaria. The Ptolemies also took a hand in some places, and in Transjordan Amman was renamed Philadelphia by one of these rulers.

Reference has already been made to the ruins at 'Araq el Emir in Transjordan, where the rock-cut tomb of one of the Tobiahs carries an inscription in Aramaic. The building in the vicinity, called by some a mausoleum and by others a palace, was built in a vigorous Hellenistic style with carved lions and Corinthian capitals. More recently it has been argued that we have here the remains of a fortress. It was built of huge blocks of limestone and was set upon a slight elevation, surrounded by a small lake, and nearly completely surrounded by walls.[18] This whole building is probably to be referred to the time of Hyrcanus, the last of the Tobiads, for Josephus[19] described the layout in great detail and credited it to Hyrcanus who, he says, lived across the Jordan and built this remarkable place for himself. If that is so, the building would date from about 175 B.C., just before the days of the Maccabees.[20]

The town of Bethzur is full of interest because it provides an interesting correlation between the documentary evidence and the excavated evidence. It was the scene of several battles during the Maccabean wars. The earliest town here was probably built during the Persian period as a protection for the Jews against the Idumeans. In the days of the Ptolemies, it was a prosperous place, to judge from the range of coins found in the excavation. Fifty-two coins from the days of the first six Ptolemies were brought to light, the earliest dating to 252 B.C. and the latest to 210 B.C. There were other coins found in the site, but they tell a different story.[21] There were in all

18. C. C. McCown, *op. cit.*, pp. 66, 68.
19. Josephus, *Antiquities* XII, iv, 11.
20. W. F. Albright, *Archaeology of Palestine* (London, 1956), pp. 149, 150.

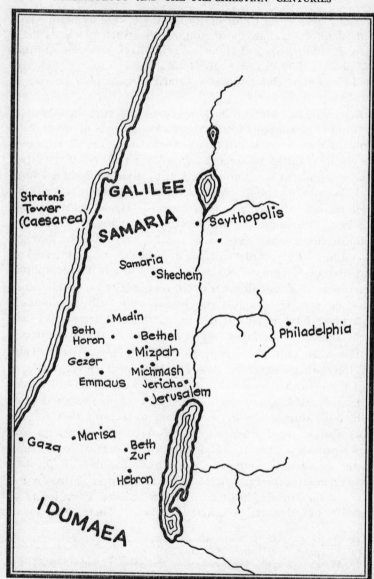

Straton's Tower (Caesarea)

GALILEE

SAMARIA

Scythopolis

Samaria
Shechem

Madin

Beth Horon
Bethel
Mizpah

Gezer
Michmash
Emmaus
Jericho
Jerusalem

Philadelphia

Gaza
Marisa
Beth Zur

Hebron

IDUMAEA

DAYS OF THE MACCABEES.

nearly three hundred coins found in the excavation, but the greater part of them come from the days of the Seleucids and the Maccabees. In detail, the story is as follows. There were 126 coins of Antiochus Epiphanes (175-163 B.C.), none from his successor, 5 from Balas (150-145 B.C.), 13 from Demetrius II (145-139 B.C.),10 from Antiochus VII (139-129 B.C.), only 2 Seleucid coins from the years 125-121 B.C., but 16 Jewish ones from the days of John Hyrcanus the Jewish ruler (134-104 B.C.). This story in coins tells us that Bethzur was occupied in the days of Antiochus IV, with a decline in occupation between 160 and 145 B.C. There was a revival, then, from 145 B.C. till late in the reign of John Hyrcanus. After about 100 B.C. the coin story ceases.

On the summit of the mound of Bethzur the excavators discovered the foundations of a large fortress which gave evidence of three periods of occupation. The first, built in the days of the Ptolemies, was almost completely destroyed and re-built into a much larger fortress. It can be attributed to Judas Maccabeus, who built it between 165 and 163 B.C. Soon after it was captured, destroyed and rebuilt on a Hellenistic plan by the Seleucid general Bacchides about 161 B.C.[22] The archaeological picture thus follows closely the literary picture.

The coin story shows a gap in occupation again till 145 B.C., which takes us to the days of Jonathan and Simon, when the fortress again fell into the hands of the Jews.

One interesting sidelight on the excavations in Bethzur is that there was a considerable collection of jar handles from large wine jars that normally came from Rhodes, and which have become known as Rhodian jar handles. Each of these bears the name of the potter or magistrate for the year. The presence of so many of these here testifies to a Greek garrison

21. O. R. Sellars and W. F. Albright, "The first campaign of Excavation at Beth-Zur," *Bulletin of the American Schools of Oriental Research*, No. 43, p. 10.
22. W. F. Albright, *Archaeology of Palestine* (London, 1956), pp. 151-152.

in the town, and as G. E. Wright says, "They certainly preferred this imported wine to the native product of the local vintage."[23]

Our next site, the town of Gezer, was finally taken by Simon. It was in a strategic position, guarding the approaches to Judea from the west and commanding the great coast road. From the literature we learn that the town was taken after a desperate struggle, and the heathen population deported and replaced by Jewish colonists. Then Simon "made it stronger than it was before and built therein a dwelling place for himself" (I Macc. 13:43-48). An important inscription [24] found in the debris reads,

Pampras says: May fire overtake Simon's palace.

This Pampras, with a Greek name, was probably one of those dispossessed by Simon, and left a curse scratched on a wall.

Ruins at Gezer were interpreted by R. A. S. Macalister as a Maccabaean castle, but more recently Y. Yadin[24a] has shown them to be the remains of a Solomonic gate. However, the Maccabaean town has been exposed and among other interesting features in the town was a building which seems to have been a town bath house. It was built of stone, lined with cement, with benches around the walls, a drain beneath the floor, and a heating room at one end. It is possible, however, that the building was some sort of industrial plant.

We have already made reference to the town of Marisa,[25] the site of the Moresheth-gath of the Old Testament (Josh. 15:44, Micah 1:15, Jer. 26:18, etc.). Excavations gave Ptolemaic coins, showing occupation at that time. During the days of the Seleucids the town was in the hands of these hated foreigners (II Macc. 12:32ff.), until it finally fell into the hands of the Jews during the reign of John Hyrcanus about 110 B.C.

23. G. E. Wright, *Biblical Archaeology* (London, 1957), p. 209, col. 1.

24. R. A. Macallister, *Gezer I*, pp. 211-12.

24a. Y. Yadin, "Solomon's City Wall and Gate at Gezer," *Israel Exploration Journal*, Vol. 8, pp. 80ff.

25. See above, pp. 86, 87.

Samaria was an important town during the Greek period and there are several indications of Greek occupation here. Some 2000 Rhodian jar handles, for example, are a strong testimony to the presence of Greek soldiers.[26] In the actual building remains we may refer to the fine Hellenistic wall built astride the earlier Israelite wall, and especially the magnificent round towers which are dated nowadays to the time of Alexander the Great, who settled Greek colonists there. His representative Perdiccas is said to have rebuilt Samaria.[27] He repaired the old Israelite walls and strengthened them by these round towers. There is a line of walls built around the summit of the mound about four metres thick, which is dated about 150 B.C. and points to the time of the Maccabean troubles. The town of Samaria fell finally to the sons of John Hyrcanus, when a ditch was built around the city as well as a double line of walls, to starve the people out. All relief from Syria was cut off and Samaria returned at last to Jewish hands in 107 B.C.

The town of Shechem suffered a violent destruction during the course of these years and it has been conjectured that this may have been due to John Hyrcanus in 128 B.C. It was, however, reoccupied and continued to be used till about 100 B.C. A coin of Antiochus VIII dated about 121-120 B.C. and another from 112-111 B.C. point to an occupation of Shechem extending into the period of Jewish freedom which preceded the Roman occupation.[28]

EVIDENCE FROM THE PERIOD 135 B.C. TO 63 B.C.

When Simon was foully slain at the instigation of his son-in-law, his son John Hyrcanus who was governor at Gezer came at once to Jerusalem and took over control of the government. In 130 B.C. he was attacked by the Seleucid ruler Antiochus VII, who was making a bold bid to regain control over Judah. He

26. G. E. Wright, *Biblical Archaeology* (London, 1957), p. 209.
27. W. F. Albright, *Archaeology of Palestine* (London, 1956), p. 150.
28. G. E. Wright, "The Second Campaign at Tell Balatah (Shechem)," *Bulletin of the American Schools of Oriental Research*, Dec. 1957, No. 148, pp. 27-28.

actually succeeded momentarily and took John Hyrcanus off to Mesopotamia to war against the Parthian hordes, who were becoming a menace at this time. Very soon Antiochus died and John was free. He returned to Jerusalem and reigned there for thirty years during which time he extended the boundaries of Judah greatly. He was able to take Shechem, subdue the Samaritans and the Idumeans and, as we have seen, retake Samaria by the hands of his two sons. He was keen to proselytize neighboring peoples and forced many to be circumcised. He was high priest as well as ruler, and offended many by his carelessness in the priestly office and by his political ambition. He offended such new groups as the Pharisees, for example. In order to provide some protection against the Seleucids he strengthened the links with Rome. His reign saw the start of tension between two groups that we later know as the Pharisees and the Sadducees.

John's successor was his son, who took the title King, but he reigned only one year as Aristobulus I. It was a busy year and he kept his brothers out of the way by casting them into prison. On his death in 103 B.C., his brother Alexander Jannaeus (103-76 B.C.) succeeded him and married his widow, much to the disgust of the pious groups. He turned out to be an ambitious and successful ruler, but he was cruel and unpopular. Although he extended the boundaries of Judah still further to the east of Galilee, and into Philistia and central Transjordan, he had serious clashes with the religious groups, and especially with the Pharisees. It was in this general period that the sect of Qumran, to be discussed in the next chapter, founded their monastery in the wilderness near the Dead Sea. Before Alexander died he advised his wife to divide the priestly and the kingly functions. This she did, ruling the country herself as Alexandra (76-67 B.C.), and having her son Hyrcanus appointed high priest. On her death the weak Hyrcanus remained high priest and the other son, Aristobulus, was king. Trouble arose when Hyrcanus fell under the influence of an Idumean named Antipater whose father had been appointed governor of Idumea by Alexander Jannaeus. A master of intrigue, the younger Antipater provoked trouble between the two brothers by persuading Hyrcanus to exert his claim to the throne. The neighboring Nabataean king was called in to help, and the Jews were in two hostile camps. In such circumstances the Roman general Pompey, at the time in Syria, stepped in to settle the matter. In the end, Aristobulus was taken to Rome, Hyrcanus was allowed to remain as high priest and was given the title of ethnarch, while the wily Antipater continued as an agent of the Romans, in the capacity of an adviser, until he was murdered in 43 B.C.

These years, from the accession of John Hyrcanus to the conquest by the Romans, have left some archaeological material. The town of Bethel was occupied during this period and has yielded coins of John Hyrcanus, Alexander Jannaeus, and later rulers, but a lack of coins from the time of Herod suggests a period of non-occupation.

Tell en Nasbeh tells a similar story, although it was occupied in Herod's time. One of the greatest hoards of coins yet found in Palestine comes from Joppa where, in 1949, some 851 coins of Alexander Jannaeus were unearthed, all of them of one type, bearing the inscription "Alexander, King." There was evidently a mint at Joppa which supplied coins for Alexander.[29]

The final collapse of Samaria came during these years, and other towns like Marisa and Bethshan fell to the Hasmonean kings. We have reviewed the archaeological material for these towns above. One general feature for the three towns, Bethzur, Gezer, and Marisa, is that the series of Jewish coins comes to an end about 100 B.C. The reason is not clear, but it may mean that soon after the aggressive policy of Alexander Jannaeus (103-76 B.C.) these towns were abondoned because it was no longer necessary to maintain garrisons at these points.[30]

It is of considerable interest to us to follow the story of

29. A. Kindler, "The Jaffa Hoard of Alexander Jannaeus," *Israel Exploration Journal*, Vol. 4, 1954, pp. 170ff.
30. W. F. Albright, *Archaeology of Palestine* (London, 1956), pp. 153-154.

the coins of the Hasmonean rulers through these years. A letter from a Seleucid ruler, referred to in I Maccabees 15:6, tells how Simon was given leave to coin money. There is some debate about whether certain coins that have been found are really to be attributed to Simon or not. One recent writer suggests that it was only after the death of Antiochus VII in 129 B.C., when the Seleucid power in Palestine was finally broken, that Maccabean coinage began to be minted.[31] It is clear that John Hyrcanus (134-104 B.C.) did make coins, using as symbols on their face flowers, fruit, stars, anchors, and such items as would not offend a people that held to the divine authority of the second commandment. On the reverse side he commonly used the cornucopia, the pomegranate, and a wreath, with the inscription in archaic Hebrew letters reading, "John the High Priest and the Community of the Jews." One of the common coins was the tiny bronze *lepton,* which was made in Judah more than any other coin. It is the widow's mite of which the value was one four-hundredth part of a shekel.

Alexander Jannaeus had the title "King" put on his coins, and used Greek letters on some of them as well as the old Hebrew letters. His symbols were the palm, the lily, the pomegranate, the cornucopia, and the wheel. By the time of Hyrcanus II (63 B.C. ff.) the coins bear only the title "High Priest," but by then the Romans were in control. The last of the Hasmoneans was Antigonus, who seized the throne in 40 B.C., at the time when the Roman Empire was in a turmoil. In the years immediately preceding the appointment of Herod as king, Antigonus actually had coins minted with the title "King Antigonus" on one side, and the words "Mattathias, the High Priest and the Communty of the Jews" on the other. These coins were significant because they give us the Jewish name of Antigonus. They were, however, poor coins, being seriously adulterated, with twenty-seven percent copper, thus reflecting the deterioration due to Roman extortions and con-

31. L. Kadman, "The Hebrew Coin Script," *Israel Exploration Journal,* Vol. 4, p. 150.

tinual warfare. The symbols on these coins were the usual ones, but in addition we now find for the first time the seven-branched candlestick that was to become so common in later synagogue art.

We might be permitted to make one concluding remark to this chapter. It is that although the archaeological evidence, apart from the magnificent finds at Qumran and in other areas nearby, is by no means spectacular, our knowledge of these times is provided by a good deal of written evidence for most of this period, particularly for the latter part, thanks to writers like Josephus. To a large extent Greek remains lie near the surface of the mounds and tells of Palestine, and have either eroded away or have been removed for the buildings of the Romans, Arabs, and later builders. Nevertheless, such material as is available is of considerable value in supplementing the written records.

CHAPTER SIX

THE RELIGIOUS COMMUNITY OF QUMRAN

IT WAS DURING the Greek period we have been discussing that a remarkable community of Jews settled in the barren hills to the west of the northern end of the Dead Sea. The sect flourished here from the last part of the second century B.C. until about 70 A.D., living, so it seems, partly in a monastery whose remains have now been excavated, and partly in the caves nearby. Valuable manuscripts were left behind by these people, to be discovered in recent years and thus to provide the world with what is in some ways the most spectacular archaeological discovery of our times.

When Muhammed ed Dhib, a young Bedouin shepherd, threw a stone into a small circular hole in a cliff in these hills bordering the Dead Sea, and heard something crack and break, he could have had no idea of the train of excitement he was to set in motion in the lands far away to the west. He had discovered a treasure trove of ancient manuscripts, the like of which had never been found before, and which was but the prelude to yet other discoveries of a similar kind. Since that first exciting discovery in perhaps March 1947, each year has brought to light yet more amazing discoveries. Now that we have the story unfolded, at least in part, we can reconstruct the setting with some clarity. We shall do this in order to make the significance of the find clearer.

HELLENIZATION AND THE PIOUS JEWS OF THE SECOND CENTURY B.C.

In our last chapter we outlined the growth of the Greek influence in Palestine to the point where it led to a Jewish revolt. It was an influence that began back in the fifth century B.C., when Greek traders visited the land and Greek influences in agriculture, coinage, pottery, art, thought, ways of living, indeed in nearly every aspect of life, were imbibed by the people of Palestine. Then came the days of the Ptolemies and the Seleucids, who had the specific intention in most cases of Hellenizing the East. The Jews themselves were divided in their reaction to these influences, for, although on the purely cultural level Greek ways might be acceptable, there were dangers for the spiritual life of the Jews. Acceptance of Greek influence in some areas was likely to lead to repercussions in other areas, and perhaps finally to a destruction of the Jewish way of life, which, after all, was based on the very law of God. Pious men who became known as the Hasidim banded together to resist these sinister influences. When Antiochus IV (Epiphanes) came to the Seleucid throne in 175 B.C. he, too, had the policy of Hellenizing the East and so providing a unifying force for his empire. Because of this he soon interfered with the legitimate priesthood of the Jews, replacing the descendant of Zadok by Menelaus, who was sworn to assist the progress of Hellenization. Antiochus finally decided to prohibit the distinctive features of the Jewish faith, and this led, as we have seen, to the Maccabean revolt. Many Jews were slain, others resisted by fighting back. It was 142 B.C. before the pagans were finally driven out by the efforts of the Maccabean leaders. At first these leaders were supported by the Hasidim, who were anxious above all else to secure religious liberty, but once this had been obtained they were not at all interested in the political aspirations of the Hasmonean family, and they withdrew their support. A particular evil from their point of view was that the Hasmonean family had taken the position of high priest as a gift from the pagan Seleucid rulers, and had then endeavored to combine with it political ambitions. When finally Aristobulus I took the title King, and Alexander Jannaeus seemed to go into the depths of wickedness, many of the Hasidim seem to have organized themselves into a group to resist such evils. From such a setting the

Pharisees were to emerge. One of the groups found a leader whom they called the *Teacher of Righteousness*,[1] withdrew into the wilderness of Judea, and organized themselves into a religious community in the region of what we know today as Wadi Qumran.

There are perhaps some elements of conjecture in the story as we have outlined it here, but it is essentially correct. Archaeologically some important points have been established. The record of coins found at Qumran starts with the coins of John Hyrcanus (134-104 B.C.), and it continues until the time of Antigonus (40-37 B.C.). There was a break at this point, with a lack of evidence from the days of Herod the Great, but the story resumes in the reign of his son Archelaus (4 B.C.-A.D. 6), and carries on till about 70 A.D., when there is another break. Finally, there are some coins from the period 132-135 A.D.

It appears that the site was abandoned about 37 B.C. for a reason that is not yet known. An earthquake wrecked a good deal of the building in 31 B.C., but after Herod's death the people returned and stayed then till 70 A.D., at which time the Romans finally devastated the place. It was at this period, when the Roman legions were moving towards Qumran, that we think that the inhabitants hid their precious documents in the caves nearby, hoping to return later. But they never did. The last occupation in the days of the second Jewish revolt was a Roman one. Although this strange community had come to an end, the nature of the people and of their beliefs and hopes were carefully portrayed for us in their documents.

WRITTEN TREASURES FROM THE CAVES OF QUMRAN

The first cave that was entered produced a number of amazing documents, some of which were acquired by the Syrian monks in Jerusalem, and others by the Hebrew University of the State of Israel. The main documents were a complete roll

---

1. Or "Right Teacher." See T. H. Gaster, *The Dead Sea Scriptures* (New York, 1957), p. 5.

of the book of Isaiah, a second roll of Isaiah complete from chapter 41 onwards but with fragments of earlier chapters, a commentary on the first two chapters of Habakkuk, the Rule of the Community, an expanded Aramaic paraphrase of Genesis, chapters 5 to 15, a book now known as the *Wars of the Children of Light Against the Children of Darkness,* and a book of Thanksgiving Psalms.

These finds were startling enough, and they may be followed up by the reader in some of the excellent accounts now available,[2] but they were only a start. The cave from which these original documents came was subsequently discovered in January 1949 by trained archaeologists, and a systematic search was undertaken by experts in February to March 1949. Unauthorized persons had been there before them, and had disturbed the cave a good deal, but many fragments were found on the floor of the cave, including scraps of Genesis, Leviticus, Deuteronomy, Judges, Samuel, Isaiah, Ezekiel, Psalms. There were also portions of commentaries on Micah, Zephaniah, and Psalms, all in very fragmentary form, and some pieces of other books, such as the Book of Noah, the Book of Jubilees and the Testament of Levi.

Towards the end of 1951 a second cave was found by the Bedouin, containing yet more fragments, which they sold to the Museum in Jerusalem. At once an expedition of scholars set off to search the area. They were able to investigate forty caves. It was in March 1952 that pottery of the type found in the first cave was found in several others, pointing to occupation by the same people at about the same time. Two of the caves (Cave 2 and Cave 3), contained fragments of the Old Testament, but Cave 3 yielded strange inscribed copper rolls, which were subsequently found to contain mysterious lists of treasures and the places where they were buried.

2. F. F. Bruce, *Second Thoughts on the Dead Sea Scrolls* (Grand Rapids, 1956), Millar Burrows, *The Dead Sea Scrolls* (London, 1956), C. T. Fritsch, *The Qumran Community* (New York, 1956), Yigael Yadin, *The Message of the Scrolls* (London, 1957), J. M. Allegro, *The Dead Sea Scrolls* (London, 1957).

Cave 4 was the most startling of all in some respects, for here in September 1952 the archaeologists cleared a cave that had been disturbed by the Bedouin. It contained many thousands of pieces representing over 300 books, Biblical and non-Biblical, including every book in the Old Testament except the book of Esther. Commentaries on Psalms and Daniel and some of the minor prophets were represented, as well as hymns, apocryphal and apocalyptic writings, and fragments of other books known from Cave 1.[3]

Cave 5 was found in September 1952 also, but the archaeologists themselves were the discoverers this time. It yielded a good harvest of non-Biblical works in fragments, as well as some phylacteries.

Cave 6, high up in the cliffs behind the settlement, had some pieces of manuscripts, but the most interesting item here was a fragment of a work known as *The Damascus Document of the Sons of Zadok,* which was discovered earlier in this century in an old synagogue in Cairo. It is evident that the Qumran people knew this writing and had a copy of it in their library.

Caves 7 to 10 were found by the archaeologists, but contained very little material. Then early in 1956 Cave 11 was discovered by the Bedouin.[4] It contained material comparable in quality to that found in the first cave, including a small roll of Psalms, many pieces of the *Apocalypse of Jerusalem,* an Aramaic Targum of Job, and two copies of the book of Daniel already known in fragment form from caves 1, 4, and 6.

In addition to the work in the caves near Qumran, the excavation of the ancient ruin which represented the original monastery of the sect was undertaken. The work began in November 1951, and soon it revealed a connection between Cave 1 and the ruins when a jar of the same type as was found in the first cave came to light, along with pottery and

3. The contents of the various caves can be found in *Revue Biblique* for the years 1953ff. See also, F. F. Bruce, *op. cit.,* p. 31, and J. M. Allegro, *op. cit.,* pp. 35-40.
4. Editorial in *Evangelical Quarterly,* Oct.-Dec. 1957, pp. 193-194.

coins of the first century A.D. In the spring of 1953, 1954, 1955, and 1956 this work went on. The excavations revealed a building that had experienced three periods of occupation. Its dimensions and plan are now known.[5] Pottery and coins assist in dating the periods of occupation. The building had a water supply which came in by way of a conduit from springs in the hills behind. A considerable number of cisterns and more shallow receptacles for holding water links up with statements in the writings which show that these people had a great emphasis on ritual washings. One room in the monastery was evidently the scriptorium where the scrolls were written, for here were found the remains of benches where men sat, and even two of the inkwells. The whole building was a complex one with many rooms. It was here that the members of this strange community lived and worked to produce the manuscripts and rolls found in the caves.[6]

Quite apart from the finds directly connected with the Qumran community, there were important discoveries in other areas of the wilderness of Judea. As early as January 1952 there was a six-week campaign of excavation in the Wadi Murabba'at, eleven miles to the south, which produced evidence of occupation in the Chalcolithic age (before 4000 B.C.), the Middle Bronze Age (2000-1550 B.C.), the Iron Age (1200-550 B.C.), and the Roman period. In all, four caves were investigated. The texts, coming mostly from the second cave, were of various types. One non-Biblical text in Hebrew was written over an earlier text probably in the centuries B.C., while other texts came from the post-Christian centuries. Some fragments of Genesis, Exodus, Deuteronomy, and Isaiah were from the first and second centuries A.D. Included among the finds were also a complete phylactery, several ostraca, and a sensational find of two letters of the leader of the second Jewish

5. The overall area was some 260 feet square.
6. Details are to be found in J. T. Milik, *Dix ans de découvertes dans le désert de Juda* (Paris, 1957), pp. 41-44 and diagram 3. See also R. de Vaux, "Fouilles au Khirbet Qumran," *Revue Biblique*, Jan. 1953, pp. 83-106.

revolt of 135 A.D., the well-known Bar Kochba, whose real name, as revealed by the letters, was Simon ben Kosebah. In the same caves were fragments of Latin and Arabic manuscripts. None of these finds is to be related in any way to the Qumran material.

In yet another area, in the Wadi en Nar, which is the extension of the Brook Kedron, a ruined site was investigated in February to April 1953. It yielded fragments of Greek New Testament texts, as well as Syro-Palestinian and Arabic texts. The place was formerly an early Christian monastery, now known as Khirbet Mird.

As a result of all this searching and excavation, scholars have an embarrassing wealth of material which will occupy them in close study for many years to come. Not only do the finds throw light on the remarkable religious community of Qumran, but they also give valuable information about the thought of those times, the character of the Hebrew text, the background to the ferment of Biblical interpretation in which our Lord Jesus Christ preached and in which the Christian Church was formed, as well as insight into various aspects of the history of those times. We shall comment briefly on some of these items, indicating the lines which should be followed up by the thoughtful reader.

THE CHARACTER OF THE QUMRAN COMMUNITY

The written material discovered in the caves, and especially the *Manual of Discipline,* or the *Rule of the Community* as some writers now call it, enables us to obtain a fairly clear impression of the basic ideas, the constitution, and the practice of the community.[7]

In the difficult days of the last part of the second century B.C. the pious group of Jews represented here was convinced that the end of this wicked age was at hand and that days of judgment spoken of by the prophets of the Old Testament

---

7. Simple outlines are to be found in F. F. Bruce, *op. cit.*, pp. 99-111, and T. H. Gaster, *op. cit.*, pp. 1-28.

were about to commence. The very site of the monastery was at the point where the river described in Ezekiel, chapter 47, entered the Dead Sea. In such perilous times this society believed that God still had a remnant of faithful people, who were in the line of the faithful remnants of past days, but that this one was the final one. The people of Qumran used names for themselves which remind us of the names of God's covenant people in the Old Testament, such as "the Elect," "the Saints of the Most High," "the Sons of Light," "the Holy People," "the Poor of the Flock," and "the Community of Israel and Aaron." As members of the Covenant they believed that they were already in possession of the Law of God, but they desired to live by its precepts. Their great aim was to study the Torah in order to discover its true interpretation along lines of procedure that had been given to them by the Teacher of Righteousness (or Right Teacher),[8] who had set out for them the way of holiness and had showed them how to live and to serve God in such momentous days. They now awaited the dawning of the Messianic age in which there would be a new Jerusalem and a new Temple, where worthy sacrifices would be offered by a worthy priesthood. Until that day dawned, this community of God's Elect was required to devote itself to the Law of God, to submit to the discipline of the sect, and even be prepared to suffer as an atonement for the sins of Israel that had gone astray. Indeed, they would make atonement for the whole earth and thus bring wickedness to an end.

The community was organized rather like a medieval monastery, with members composed of both the priests (sons of Zadok) and laity. At the head of the hierarchy stood the priests, who were supreme in all matters, doctrinal and economic, and after them the Levites, the elders, and the rest of the people. The laity was divided into groups of thousands,

8. F. F. Bruce, *The Teacher of Righteousness in the Qumran Texts* (London, 1957), has an excellent summary of present knowledge about this figure.

hundreds, fifties, and tens, and the priests had authority over them in matters of law and property. Yet all members of the community were allowed to vote on matters of law and property in the General Assembly which was conducted according to certain fixed rules. The priests in the Assembly took their places first, then the elders, then the rest. No one was allowed to speak while his brother was speaking, and the Supervisor who presided gave each man a clear opportunity to speak.

There was another important group, the Council, a sort of Supreme Court, comprising twelve men, of whom three were priests, all skilled in the Law, "to guard faithfulness in the land."

It seems that there were organized cells of this sect wherever ten men were found belonging to the order. Of these, one needed to be a priest who was able to interpret the Law to them at any time of day or night, so as to preserve harmony.

It was not easy to become a member of this community. A man had to volunteer, and to agree to live by the regulations of the sect. He was first examined by the Overseer as to his intelligence and character. After a time he appeared before the "many" and was examined. He was then required to serve a full year of probation during which he did not share either in the wealth of the community or in the purifactory rites. At the end of the year he was examined again, and if accepted, he deposited his property with the Overseer, and was allowed the next year to share the purifactory rites of the group, but not its communal meal. When finally he was accepted, he surrendered all his property, which was merged in the common fund, and after confession, and the reciting of blessings and curses by the priests, the applicant became a full member of the Covenant Community. He swore to follow the law of Moses, to live by it and to shun all evil men and their ways.

Communal life was expressed in various ways. The two principal rites were baptism and the communal meal, and in these all members had a part. There were many occasions on which members of the sect had to carry out ritual washings, not only at their initial baptism but also on various other occasions which required outward lustrations. The community did not regard these washings as in themselves a substitute for purity of heart, and several portions in their writings insist on inward purity as the only way to win divine approval. The outward washing was only the symbol of inward cleansing.

The communal meal was another occasion where the whole group acted in unison, and where "all are to dine together, worship together and take counsel together."[9] When they ate, the priest occupied the first place, and after that the members sat in their orders. Before meals, which evidently had a sacramental character, the priest gave thanks. In other ways, too, the society was communal. There was a good deal of work to be done on this basis, covering a great variety of occupations, so that the group could gain its daily bread. The excavations revealed the potters' corner and the room where the scribes worked, and it is believed that there is evidence of farming activity also in the area.

Time to these men was a sacred trust from God, and there were set times for prayer and meditation as well as for work. Throughout the night some of the men were engaged in the study of the Torah, the Law of God, in three shifts. Wherever ten men were gathered, one of them devoted himself to the study of the law exclusively.

There were penalties imposed on those who broke the laws and offended in matters of community discipline. These were, for the most part, exclusion from the fellowship and reduction of the food ration. Details can readily be found in the *Manual of Discipline*.

It would appear that women as well as men might be admitted to the community, and that marriage and family life were not discouraged. The graves in the area gave evidence of the presence of women in the community, for a number of female skeletons was found and there are references in the

9. T. H. Gaster, *op. cit.*, p. 49; *Manual of Discipline*, col. vi, lines 2, 3.

documents to both women and children. The sect often took children in from outside and trained them along with other children for a period of ten years, after which the young adult could apply for membership in the society for which he was eligible at the age of twenty, admittance being in the usual way, after examination and probation. Charles T. Fritsch has given an excellent summary of the character of the Qumran sect.[10]

> The Qumran sect was a monastic community whose members practiced the common life according to strict regulations; it was a covenant community which lived according to the requirements of the New Covenant; it was a sacramental community in that every phase of life was lived in accordance with the divine ordinances; it was a priestly community in that its life was directed by priests, or sons of Zadok; it was a Bible-centered community where the Scriptures were read and studied day and night, and where Biblical texts were continually copied by members of the group; and finally, it was an apocalyptic community, waiting expectantly for the quick overthrow of evil and the establishment of God's kingdom here on earth.

We may suspect that the first settlers at Qumran believed the end to be very near, and no doubt they thought the time had come when the Romans came to the land in 63 B.C., for it seems certain that the Romans feature in their writings as one of the factors in the final victory. However, for a reason that is not clear, they vacated their settlement for some years and departed to "Damascus," returning after the death of Herod to await the time of the end. During these years John the Baptist was declaring that the time had come, and that Jesus Christ was the Messiah. This teaching did not influence the Qumran sect, and they were still in their monastery in 68 A.D. when the Roman armies began to quell the revolt of the Jews who were led by the more violent elements of the nation, anxious to hasten on the downfall of the Romans. In the reprisals that followed the whole of Judah was subdued and along with it the Qumran settlement was destroyed. In a sense

10. C. T. Fritsch, *op. cit.*, p. 75.

the end had come, but not in the way the community had hoped for.

THE QUMRAN APPROACH TO THE OLD TESTAMENT

The Qumran community believed that God had given them special insight into the meaning of the Old Testament scriptures, which were interpreted so as to enable the readers to see in the scriptures a description of their own times and circumstances. This became evident to modern scholars from the earliest days of the finds, for the commentary on Habakkuk, one of the rolls in the first cave, followed just these lines. The interpreter ignored the historical meaning of the text, and read into it the present evil age, so that the text became a source of guidance for the present, an approach not unusual even in our own days. If the reader will take up one of the popular translations of the texts, and read the commentary on Habakkuk or Nahum, he will see that the method is to quote the Bible text and then add the words, "The interpretation of this concerns . . . ."[11] Sometimes the phrase used to introduce the interpretation may differ slightly from this, but the meaning of the passage for "today" is stated after the Bible text in each case.

All of this material is valuable for us today, because it throws light on the history of the times. Unfortunately at the present time we are still in the dark about the meaning of some of the references. For example, reference to the Kittim, which occurs in more than one place, seems to point to the Romans, but there are still some scholars who think differently, and we shall need more information before we can finally decide. When once the picture becomes clear, we shall have valuable material for dating the age at which these documents were written. Present indications are that the date of composition was between 135 B.C. and 70 A.D. That this approach to the interpretation of the Old Testament was used quite regularly seems to be implied by the fact that we now have this type of com-

11. T. H. Gaster, *op. cit.*, pp. 229-261. Millar Burrows, *op. cit.*, pp. 365-370.

mentary for quite a number of Old Testament books, but notably the prophets.

THE QUMRAN COMMUNITY AND THE MESSIAH

The two centuries before the Christian era were centuries of speculation in many ways, as a study of the apocryphal, pseudepigraphic, and apocalyptic literature of those centuries will show. Such themes as the Messiah, the Day of the Lord, the final Judgment, the lot of the wicked, were taken up by many writers, and the Qumran Community, born in the midst of this sort of speculation, reflected the discussion of the day. There were, however, some novel ideas. The people believed that things would go on as they were, till "the coming of a prophet and the anointed ones [Messiahs] of Aaron and Israel,"[12] and it was these duly anointed persons, one a high priest and one a king, for whom the community waited. Thus, they expected a prophet, a priest, and a king in that day. One document from Cave 4 showed that the teachers of Qumran made use of several passages from the Old Testament to justify their Messianic ideas. Here were collected Deuteronomy 18:18-19, which refers to a prophet, Numbers 24:15-17, which refers to a king, and Deuteronomy 33:8-11, where Moses pronounced his blessing on the priestly tribe of Levi. The whole society was called "the community of Israel and Aaron," and it evidently expected the two Messiahs to emerge from its own ranks. In another of the documents, the order of precedence of those who sit down at the banquet in the new age is given, and here the Messiah of Israel is subordinate to the Priest. We are reminded of the inferior position of the Prince in the latter chapters of Ezekiel. It is noteworthy, in the light of these unusual Messianic ideas, that in Christianity the three figures of prophet, priest, and king are united in our Lord Jesus Christ whose Messiahship was achieved through the suffering of the cross.[13]

    12. F. F. Bruce, *op. cit.*, p. 77, and *Rule of Community*, col. ix, line 11. Compare T. H. Gaster, *op. cit.*, p. 58.
    13. F. F. Bruce, *op. cit.*, pp. 76-84.

THE SCROLLS AND THE TEXT OF THE OLD TESTAMENT

Prior to the discovery of these texts, our earliest Hebrew manuscripts were dated about 900 A.D. It has always been the desire of Biblical scholars to obtain earlier manuscripts in order to make a comparison with the present-day Hebrew text. In this way they could discover how well the text has been preserved. As a result of these wonderful Qumran discoveries, we now have documents as old as 100 B.C., or perhaps even earlier.[14] How do they compare with the Massoretic text which we have in our Hebrew Bible, and which was fixed by the Rabbis according to the tradition (Massorah) which held in the early centuries of the Christian era?

A number of interesting facts has emerged. The most important is that in the main these ancient texts agree fairly closely with the text with which we are familiar. Where they diverge they not infrequently follow the Septuagint text more closely, and this diverges from the Hebrew text in a number of places. It is evident also that there were versions of the Hebrew Bible in existence in those days that differed from both the present Massoretic text and the Septuagint text.

From these discoveries, certain facts are clear. It is plain that the Massoretic text, or at least the original form of it, is quite ancient. Although the standardization took place in early Christian times, the process was going on at least in the first century B.C. At the same time it is apparent that the translators of the Septuagint had a slightly different form of the text in Egypt, but it was a form that was not unknown in Palestine, for there is evidence of it in the caves of Qumran. Furthermore, the discoveries of these recent days show that there were still other forms (recensions) of the Hebrew Bible that were current in Palestine in those centuries. It became necessary for the Jews to decide on a standard text for their own use, and this the Rabbis did quite early in Christian times.

14. F. F. Bruce, *op. cit.*, pp. 34-44; Millar Burrows, *op. cit.*, pp. 73-122. A few persistent critics still seek to deny that the documents are pre-Christian and push them into post-Christian times.

It is probably because of these different texts that were in use in the days of the early Church, that the quotations from the Old Testament occurring in the New Testament are difficult to trace exactly in many cases. Future work on the wealth of manuscript material will do much to show how our Hebrew Bible finally came into its present form.

THE QUMRAN SECT AND THE ZADOKITES

We have already made passing reference to the discovery many years ago, in an ancient synagogue in Egypt, of several fragments of a strange document which belonged to a sect of Jews known as the Karaites. The document was originally written by Jews who regarded themselves as a covenant group. Apparently they had migrated to "Damascus,"[15] where they were organized into a community by a leader called "the Star." The document found in Egypt has been called the Damascus Document or the Zadokite Fragment, because of its reference to Damascus and to the sons of Zadok. It gives details of a sect which, in many ways, resembled the sect we have come to know as the Qumran sect. The two lots of written material are related in style and terminology, and the two groups are similar in organization, in structure, and in many of their basic beliefs. Indeed, even before fragments of the Damascus Document were found at Qumran some scholars were postulating a connection between the two groups. The question naturally arose whether the Qumran people knew of the writings of the Damascus group. The discovery of fragments of this Damascus Document in Cave 6 makes it clear that the covenant community at Qumran was in possession of the rules and procedures of the Damascus or Zadokite sect. When a comparison is made between the two groups, it becomes clear that there are differences as well as resemblances. It was easier to enter the Damascus group than to enter the

15. It is not agreed by all that this term is to be taken literally. See R. North "The Damascus of Qumran Geography," *Palestine Exploration Quarterly*, 1955, pp. 34ff.

Qumran group for it was only necessary to take an oath and be enrolled by the Supervisor. In the matter of personal goods, too, the Damascus sect had easier rules, for its members were required only to give two days' wages a month to community funds. Again, this group had closer connections with the Temple in Jerusalem, although it was stricter in its observance of many of the requirements of the Law than the orthodox Jews of Jerusalem.

It seems that the two communities were closely related, if not identical. However, because of the differences, some scholars think that perhaps they represent two different stages, with the possibility that the Damascus group was the later. We cannot at this stage give a final answer as to the relationships between the two.[16]

THE QUMRAN SECT AND THE ESSENES

Several ancient writers, such as the Roman, Pliny, and the Jews, Josephus and Philo, give a good deal of detail about a sect that was in existence in their time, called the Essenes. Its members were scattered throughout Palestine and were celibates for the most part, although some did marry. They lived a very strict life, and in many ways conducted themselves like the community of Qumran. They had community meals, devoted themselves to prayer, engaged in ritual washings, were sworn to piety, and in general followed out a way of life that reminds us both of the Damascus (or Zadokite) sect and the Qumran sect. Pliny placed them in the Dead Sea area to the north of Masada and Engedi, which would bring them near to if not actually on, the site of Qumran. Josephus, however, says that they were to be found all over Palestine. There are again many resemblances between the Essenes and the Qumran sect, and also some differences. Some scholars are ready to make an outright identification of the two groups; others feel that this is not warranted at present.[17] The fact seems to

16. C. T. Fritsch, *op. cit.*, pp. 76-89.
17. F. F. Bruce, *op. cit.*, pp 112-122; C. T. Fritsch, *op. cit.*, pp. 90-110.

be emerging that there were a number of baptist and messianic groups in the Jordan Valley and in the Dead Sea area during the first centuries B.C. and A.D. John the Baptist founded one such group. It will probably turn out finally that all these groups were closely related, and traced their origins back to the same set of circumstances.

THE QUMRAN SECT AND CHRISTIANITY

In the excitement of the early days of discovery, before the written materials could be properly assessed, there were those who noticed a number of superficial resemblances between the teaching and the practices of Qumran, and those of Christianity. The conclusion was quickly formed that the origins of Christianity were to be sought in this sect. More mature consideration shows that this picture is quite false. There are vast differences between the two systems, and there is no ground at all to think that Christianity is related to the Qumran Sect.

The reason for the superficial resemblances in teaching lies in the fact that Christianity touches time and again on the range of thinking of the Jewish people of those days, and offers its own solution. The coming of the Messiah, the significance of the Old Testament for understanding the purposes of God, discussions about the Day of the Lord, the problem of the wicked and the final lot of the righteous, all of these, and many other like problems that occupied the thinking of the pious men of the times, fell for discussion among the early Christians. The writings of both the Qumran sect and of the early Christians abound in references from the Old Testament, so that similarity in language and theme by no means argues a dependence of one on the other. Both groups go back to the same basic source material in the Old Testament. There are, however, some important things to be said.

In the first place, there is at present no clear evidence of any direct contact between the Qumran community and either the founder of Christianity or the early Christians. True, such scholars as J. M. Allegro and Professor Dupont Somer have argued that in the Teacher of Righteousness we have one who anticipated the teaching, passion, and messianic claims of Jesus Christ, and that the community of Qumran was a sort of shadow of the Christian Church. These ideas have been popularized by E. Wilson,[18] but they have not met with widespread acceptance. Rather have the majority of scholars deplored the facile identification that this writer makes on the basis of insufficient evidence. The Teacher of Righteousness did not make Messianic claims for himself, nor did his followers regard him as Messiah, nor do we know how he died.

It would seem quite probable, however, that John the Baptist had contact with the Qumran sect. He lived in the deserts of Judea when he was young and finally came preaching repentance, separation from this evil age, and the practice of a life of denial, while awaiting the coming of the Messiah, whose forerunner he was (Luke 1:76-80, 3:1-8). Much of this teaching is reminiscent of the teaching of Qumran. John also baptized and spoke of judgment, but he never identified himself with the Messiah. He preached to the masses rather than to a select group of people, and when Jesus came, John recognized Him as Messiah, although he still needed to learn the fuller implications of His coming and His ministry (Matt. 11:2-6).

There seem to be many points of contact between John and the Qumran people, but if he ever did belong to the sect, we would have to conclude that he broke with them in order to follow a new path set out for him by God.[19]

When we come to Jesus Himself, we find Him living a life that was very different from that of the Covenanters of Qumran. There seem to be many parallels between His teaching and that of the Qumran sect, but this does not mean any more than that He accepted the same Scripture as they did, and lived in days when many were talking about the same great

18. E. Wilson, *The Scrolls from the Dead Sea* (London, 1957).
19. C. T. Fritsch, *op. cit.*, pp. 112-116; F. F. Bruce, *op. cit.*, pp. 128-131.

themes. It is a fact that the more we know about the literature and the discussions of these times the more we can place the teaching of Jesus in its setting, and in this regard much can be learned from the Dead Sea Scrolls. But in a thousand ways Jesus Christ was different from the people in the monastery of Qumran, both in His own life and in the peculiar emphasis of His teaching.[20] There is no trace in the teaching of this sect of those great doctrines that make Christianity really distinctive — the Incarnation, redemption through the death of One who was the Messiah, Himself Prophet, Priest, and King of Old Testament expectation, the Son of Man and the Suffering Servant alike.

There are, however, many resemblances in language and in thought between the writings of Qumran and those of the New Testament. This is only natural because the early Christians were showing how it was that Jesus Christ provided the answer to all the hopes, the strivings and the questionings of those pious souls, who, like the Covenant Community of Qumran, despaired of this present evil age. The last ten years of scholarly research on these documents have produced some thrilling discussions of the way in which Paul and others took up the challenge of the times, and showed how Christ the true Messiah had finally come in the fullness of time to make all things new.

THE IDENTITY OF PEOPLES AND EVENTS IN THE SCROLLS

We have made reference in passing to several persons who appear in the literature of the Qumran sect but there are others besides these. Such people as the Teacher of Righteousness, the Wicked Priest, the Kittim, a certain Demetrius, king of Greece, and the house of Absalom, all demand an explanation. Then some of the events referred to in the scrolls, such as the reference to the attack of the Wicked Priest, who pursued the Teacher of Righteousness to his place of exile on the Day

20. C. T. Fritsch, op. cit., pp. 116-124; F. F. Bruce, op. cit., pp. 131-137. Cf. G. Greystone, The Dead Sea Scrolls and the Originality of Christ (London, 1955).

of Atonement, will provide important clues to the true historical situation in which this literature arose. Many writers already feel that the Wicked Priest was Alexander Jannaeus (103-76 B.C.), who clashed with the Jews in his day and slew many. The Jewish rebels did invite Demetrius III, the Seleucid king at the time, to come to their aid, but just who the Teacher of Righteousness was, is not at present clear, although suggestions are not lacking. Again, the Kittim would appear to be the Romans.

The fact remains, however, that at present we are uncertain about the identification of many of the people and events referred to in the scrolls. We are confident that within a very short time now the puzzle will begin to unravel. There is such a wealth of material still being examined, and still more coming to light, that it seems inevitable that we shall soon have a solution to our problems.

It does not seem that the well-known King Herod features at all in the Qumran documents. Yet we have reason to think that he had dealings with the community there at Qumran. Archaeological evidence points to the fact that during Herod's time the monastery was deserted. The reason is not known, but it is conjectured that Herod may well have taken a strong dislike to these pious Jews so close to his Jericho palace. The Messianic teachings which they propounded could have been an offense to him and, further, the community seems to have had something of a military significance to judge from their document, *The War of the Sons of Light Against the Sons of Darkness.* If Herod set himself against them, he could do them harm, so it is quite possible that it was during these years that they went to "Damascus," to return after his death. However, here, too, we can do no more than speculate, since in any case "Damascus" may be used in a metaphorical sense, and the *War* scroll may not have referred to physical warfare any more than the Christian hymn "Onward Christian Soldiers."

It is not without good cause that many have regarded these finds in the Qumran area as the most spectacular archaeological discovery of this age. The documents have widespread significance, touching on the text of both Old and New Testaments, and on the Messianic hopes of the age and the thinking of pious men in the years surrounding the birth of the Christian Church. We feel that here we meet face to face men whose whole being is vibrant with expectation of the coming of Messiah. Even if they were wrong, and even if their interpretations of Scripture were forced and unnatural, they have left for us a strong picture of a hope which only Jesus, the true Messiah, could fulfill. The Messiahship of the Lord Jesus stands out in a thrilling contrast with the frustrated hopes of these people. And the story is not finished. We feel that much more light will yet break forth from the writings of this strange community.

CHAPTER SEVEN

THE DAYS OF HEROD THE GREAT

—————

OUR CLOSING CHAPTER will take us to the dawn of the New Testament era, for with the death of Herod the Great we are already in the days of the boyhood of Jesus of Nazareth. The exact date of His birth is still unknown, though we do know it was before the death of Herod, which was in 4 B.C. and there is some evidence that it was somewhere about 7 B.C.

With Herod's appointment as king by the Romans, after the death of Antigonus, the last of the Hasmoneans, in 37 B.C., there was a new order in Judea. Not being a true Jew, but an Idumean by birth, Herod was despised by the Jews all his days. His reign was a tragic one and he died without a friend. But because of his tremendous building program, he left behind a great deal of material which is the delight of the archaeologist today. We shall first review the history of the times and then discuss the archaeological discoveries bearing on those days.

HISTORY OF PALESTINE FROM 63 B.C. TO 4 B.C.

In 63 B.C. Pompey entered Palestine, and the Holy Land came under the direct control of Rome. This was in many ways an advantage, for it was to give the Jews peace, roads, aqueducts, and many fine buildings. Judea itself was greatly reduced in size and it was included in the Roman province of Syria, with a local governor, and Hyrcanus as high priest. Soon after, Scaurus, the Roman proconsul of Syria, had trouble with the Nabataeans, and Antipater, the father of Herod, was able to persuade the Nabataeans to pay tribute, and in this way in-gratiate himself with the Romans.

Just at this time civil strife, which was to have indirect repercussions on Palestine, was breaking out in Rome. When Gabinius became proconsul of Syria in 57 B.C. he had trouble in Judea with a Hasmonean rebel, son of the former Aris-tobulus. The revolt was quelled, and the fortresses of Alex-andrium, Hyrcania, and Machairus were demolished. In the campaign a young Roman named Antony distinguished him-self. He met the young Herod and the two became firm friends. Gabinius divided the land into five areas in order to avoid troubles. When he planned an attack on Egypt, Antipater supplied his food and water as he passed through. In 54 B.C., following the success of Gabinius in Egypt, Antipater was able to bring about the collapse of another Jewish revolt by good advice to the rebels. As a reward for his efforts he became, in effect, the ruler of the land.

By this time the Roman world was ruled by a strange alli-ance of three men called a Triumvirate, consisting of Pompey, Julius Caesar, and Licinius Crassus. In 53 B.C. Crassus met his death, and Caesar and Pompey began to fight for supreme power. Caesar won, and by 48 B.C. Pompey was dead. In Pal-estine, intrigue among the descendants of the Hasmoneans led to serious conflict, and the one man who finally profited by it all was Antipater. Whereas formerly he supported Pompey, now he supported Caesar, who at the time was need-ing help in Egypt. He was able to send 3000 Jewish troops and to persuade other Jews to assist. Hyrcanus the high priest accompanied him to Egypt. Caesar was well pleased and con-firmed Hyrcanus as ethnarch of Judea and high priest, while Antipater was made a Roman citizen and appointed to the position of procurator of Judea. He proceeded to rebuild the walls of Jerusalem, and to appoint his son Phasael prefect of Jerusalem, and his son Herod as governor of Galilee.

At once Herod proved his skill in battle and in the affairs of government. Because he executed a Jewish rebel, named Hezekiah, in the hills of Galilee, he was called before the

Sanhedrin. He went, accompanied by a bodyguard. Hyrcanus, knowing that the Sanhedrin was determined to put Herod to death, adjourned the case and advised Herod to flee from Jerusalem. This he did, and proceeded at once to report the incident to the Roman proconsul of Syria, who forthwith appointed him governor of Coele-Syria. This greatly increased his power, and enraged his enemies.

Then came the assassination of Caesar in March 44 B.C. The Roman senate confirmed the generous concessions Caesar had made to the Jews, but before long the proconsul of Syria, Cassius, an ambitious man, began to press the Jews for money and demanded that Antipater and his sons find it. They submitted, but earned the wrath of the Jews still more, so that when a Jewish conspirator, Malichus, arranged for the poisoning of Antipater, the nation was not grieved. Soon after, Cassius set off to Rome, hoping to gain the supreme place in the empire. Anarchy broke out in Judea, and Antigonus, the son of Aristobulus and nephew of the high priest Hyrcanus, tried to seize the power but was frustrated for a time.

Eventually Cassius was overthrown, and Antony and Octavian emerged supreme. Antony returned to Asia, where Herod had in the meantime married the grandchild of Hyrcanus, Mariamne, thus becoming a member of the royal family. When both parties in Judea appealed to Antony, he favored Herod and Phasael. It was no advantage to Herod, for Antigonus called on the aid of the Parthian invaders from Persia, a great menace to Roman power in the East, and paid the money to invade Judah. This they did, and for the time being the Romans were unable to deal with them. They put Antigonus on the throne and he ruled from 40 to 37 B.C. This man, as we have seen, had his name placed on coins.[1]

The position of Herod was desperate and he appealed to Rome for help. There were others who were bargaining with Rome at that time, but in the end Rome ignored them

1. See above, p. 98.

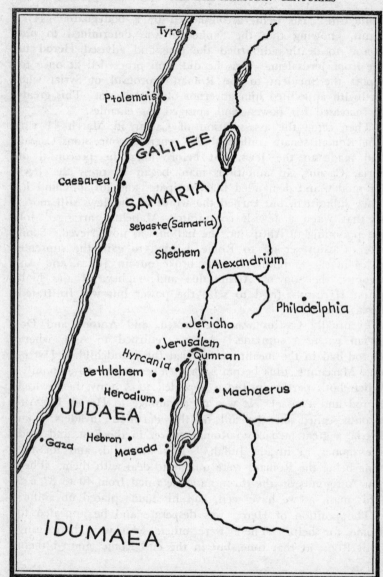

DAYS OF HEROD

all and appointed Herod as king. It took him three years to overthrow Antigonus and to enter into his possessions, but Antigonus was finally taken prisoner and executed. Thus ended the Hasmonean high priesthood.

Herod's reign can be summarized in three stages.[2] From 37 to 25 B.C. he had a good deal of strife, with serious domestic trouble, most of which he overcame by executions. When in 31 B.C. Antony was defeated by Augustus, Herod managed to obtain the goodwill of the emperor.

From 25 to 14 B.C. there was peace for the most part, during which Herod's domains were greatly enlarged as a reward for loyal service to Rome. The last years of his life were again dogged by much strife, during which he had several of his sons executed. Finally he contracted a disease and died in 4 B.C. at the age of 70.

HEROD'S BUILDING ACHIEVEMENTS

Herod was one of the most passionate builders of antiquity. Today there is a great variety of ruined buildings to be found in Palestine which date back to Herod's reign. These remains are naturally of great interest to the archaeologist. They may be classified into four groups, the Temple in Jerusalem, other buildings in Jerusalem, buildings in the rest of his kingdom, and buildings in foreign countries.[3]

Herod made use of a particular type of masonry in his buildings which has become known to the archaeologists as Herodian masonry. It consists of huge blocks of stone, generally oblong, with a smoothed-out area cut down as a margin all around the outside of the block. This is referred to technically as a marginal draft. It is quite distinctive, and can be easily recognized by the excavator. Much of his building showed a strong Hellenistic influence, and W. F. Albright has

2. S. Perowne, *The Life and Times of Herod the Great* (London, 1956).
3. *Ibid.;* cf. pp. 18-21, 115-142.

described it as the "fullest flowering of the Hellenistic architecture in Palestine."[4]

In the year 19 B.C. Herod decided to rebuild the Temple in
Jerusalem. The exact bounds of the Temple as it was when
Herod undertook his work are not known. He determined not
only to reconstruct the Temple, but also to construct a huge
courtyard in which pilgrims could gather. It was necessary to
build a platform supported by columns and vaults over a
portion of the hill to the south east where the hill fell away.
This system today is called Solomon's Stables, although it was
built by Herod. Around the platform a tremendous retaining
wall was built, sunk in places into bedrock. As early as 1867
to 1870 Sir Charles Warren excavated around the existing wall
down to bedrock. One of the best examples of the typical
Herodian masonry is to be seen at the "Wailing Wall," where
the huge blocks which make up the wall demonstrate the way
in which Herod had his masons do their work. The largest
of these blocks is 16½ feet long and 13 feet wide. In the early
part of the last century Edward Robinson found the remains
of two arches along the western side which mark the places
where bridges connected the western hill to the platform.
Unfortunately we have nothing of the Temple left today, although we suspect that if we could clear away the debris under
the stone pavements in the old Temple area we might find
some traces. We are dependent on the description of Josephus
for such details as we have. The Temple was not completed
till after Herod's death, as we learn from John 2:20. Possibly
the only items we have today coming from the Temple are a
complete and a partial inscription in Greek which forbids
Gentiles to enter the inner precincts of the Temple. They were
allowed to visit the outer court of the Temple, but they might
not penetrate into any of the inner courts on pain of death.

4. W. F. Albright, *Archaeology of Palestine* (London, 1956),
p. 154.
5. F. F. Bruce, *Commentary on the Book of the Acts* (Grand
Rapids, 1954), pp. 433-434.

The inscription discovered by Clermont-Ganneau in 1871 reads:[6]

> No foreigner may enter within the barricade which surrounds the temple and enclosure. Anyone who is caught doing so will have himself to blame for his ensuing death.

There are various other structures around Jerusalem that give evidence of Herod's work, such as the wall around the city in which he built towers, some of which he included as part of his own palace. The words of W. F. Albright give a good summary of the position today.[7]

> Almost the whole length of the Herodian First Wall of Jerusalem can be traced and remains of the Herodian masonry identified. The finest example of Herodian masonry with marginal draft, outside of the retaining wall of the Temple enclosure, appears in the so-called Tower of David at the Jaffa Gate

There are other traces of Herodian masonry in the heart of the Old City and these are important in deciding the position of the so-called Second Wall of Herod, which protected the exposed northern side of the city. Two positions are advanced, one of which leaves the Church of the Holy Sepulchre outside the wall, and the other of which leaves it inside.[8] If the site of the Church of the Holy Sepulchre is the authentic site of Calvary, this wall should allow of its being outside the city proper of Herod's day. The matter is by no means settled.

Herod also built a fortress at the northern end of the Temple and named it the Tower of Antonia after the Roman Antony. This was later to be used by Pilate as his Praetorium. It has been excavated in part in recent years, and a remarkable picture of the area has been brought to light. It contained the Gabbatha, the pavement which formed Pilate's Hall of Judgment, from which Christ was led to the cross

---

6. Details of the inscription are found in A. Deissmann, *Light from the Ancient East* (London, 1922) p. 80.

7. W. F. Albright, *op. cit.*, p. 154.

8. G. E. Wright and F. V. Filson, *Westminster Historical Atlas* (London, 1953), p. 99 and Plate XVII, c.

(John 19:13).[9]   This fortress first served as Herod's palace, but later he built a new palace to the west, referred to briefly already.   On the north side were three towers: Hippicus, named after a friend; Phasael, after his brother, and Mariamne, after his wife.   South of these lay the main palace.   Of all these, little now remains, for they were destroyed by Titus at the fall of Jerusalem in 70 A.D.   However, the so-called Tower of David probably preserves in its substructure part of the fortress of Phasael.[10]   It is possible that part of Mariamne was discovered when an Anglican Church was being built in 1901, and traces of Hippicus during the excavations of C. N. Johns between 1937 and 1948.

Of the buildings of Herod in other places in his kingdom we have today a great variety of remains available for study. One of the closest to Jerusalem was built about two miles away from the old Biblical Jericho, at the place where the Wadi Qilt opens out on to the plain.   A good water supply from springs in the Wadi made the place a delight.   Some excavation has gone on in this area and it is possible that the work of the American Schools here in 1949 and 1950[11] uncovered part of a building of Herod's time, although it had been re-used and extended by the later Arabs.   The exact nature of the original building is not easy to decide, though it may have been a palace, or a large dwelling.

But Jericho was not remote enough for Herod in his solitary moods, so he restored and re-equipped the fortresses of Alexandrium, Hyrcania, Machaerus, and Masada.   These were on high inaccessible peaks, Alexandrium high above the Jordan valley in central Palestine, Masada on the west of the Dead Sea, and Machaerus to the east, both high up and difficult to reach.   More recently Masada has been excavated in part,[12]

9. W. F. Albright, *op. cit.*, pp. 244-246.
10. *Ibid.*, p. 154.
11. *Bulletin of the American Schools of Oriental Research*, Dec., 1950, Oct., 1951.
12. H. Avi Yonah and others, "The Archaeological Survey of Masada 1955-1956," *Israel Exploration Journal*, Vol. 7, No. 1, pp. 1-60.

with some striking results. There was beauty here in the columns and general architecture. Great cisterns, storage space for food, and other remarkable features provided surprises for the excavators. There is abundant material for excavation in these fortresses, as most of them have not been touched.

One of Herod's strangest structures was the Herodium, just south of Bethlehem, where he had an artificial top put on a hill and built there a castle which was reached by two hundred steps cut in the side of the hill. The ruins at the top are still to be seen, and traces of the stairway may still be detected on the side of the hill.

Herod's work at Samaria must have been among his best. In 27 B.C. he undertook extensive work there. He first of all provided a new city wall, two and a half miles long, with towers at intervals. The chief gateway is still to be seen in ruins, with the two towers on either side. Herod called the new town Sebaste, the Greek name for Augustus, the emperor of the day, to whom this work was dedicated. Inside the wall Herod undertook the building of a magnificent temple in honor of Augustus. Built over earlier Israelite structures, it was about 225 feet square, and stood on a platform (podium), which was approached by a fine flight of stairs. Today the ruins are the most imposing of all the ruins to be seen in Samaria. The temple was high enough to view the Mediterranean Sea on a fine day. But there are other remains of interest in Samaria, such as the stadium built at the edge of the valley that runs to the north of the town, and enclosed by walls. It was 638 feet long and 190 feet across. Traces of the forum are also to be seen in the heart of the town to the east of the temple.

The town of Caesarea on the coast was another scene of Herodian activity. Here a fine port was constructed during a period of twelve years, from 25 to 13 B.C. A wall some 200 feet wide standing in 120 feet of water formed the back side of the harbor. It was made of enormous blocks of limestone, some of them 50 feet by 10 feet in size, and was furnished with towers here and there. On the shore a town was built with a semi-circular wall that enclosed the main public buildings and served to protect them. When Laurence Oliphant visited the area in 1884 he reported that "the old Roman wall could still be traced for a mile and a half enclosing an area strewn with the remains of a theatre, hippodrome, temple, aqueducts and mole."[13] Today this material has largely disappeared, but already steps are being undertaken to excavate Caesarea, both on land and in the sea.[14] Caesarea, of course, was the place where the Roman governors lived from 6 to 66 A.D. Here, too, Paul was tried before Festus and spent two years in prison. Aerial photography has revealed some important features of this famous town.

Reference may be made finally to Hebron and its surroundings, where there are a number of evidences of Herodian building. In the town itself the present Moslem mosque preserves a very fine example of Herodian masonry. One outer wall is almost completely preserved, and gives us an excellent idea of how the exterior of some of Herod's buildings would have appeared. At Ramat el Khalil, two miles to the north of Hebron, there are further examples of splendid Herodian masonry.

We shall not deal in detail with the building program of Herod in foreign lands. Among other gifts to foreign peoples we may note that he endowed Ptolemais (Acre) with a gymnasium, Damascus with a gymnasium and a theater, Sidon with a theater, Byblos with new city walls, Beirut with assembly rooms, temples, cloisters, and market place, Latakia with a new water supply, Antioch with a boulevard paved with marble and shaded with cloisters, and other towns with parks. His motive in all these seems to have been his love for art, which was restricted in Judea owing to the fact that representations of men and animals were forbidden by the commandments of Moses, and moreover no inscription could be prepared dedi-

13. S. Perowne, op. cit., p. 126.
14. Brief report in Revue Biblique, April, 1957, pp. 243-246, and various specialized discussions in recent issues of the Israel Exploration Journal.

cating an object to a man. Herod wanted to show his grati-
tude to his friends, too, and there may have been a desire also
to commend the Jews in foreign lands. This could be done, he
believed, if the ruler of the Jews showed these kindnesses to
foreigners.

OTHER ARCHAEOLOGICAL EVIDENCE FROM HEROD'S TIME

The interested student can enlarge his knowledge of the
times of Herod in other ways. It is possible, for example, by a
visit to the Museum in Jerusalem to become acquainted with
the typical pottery of the times. We have referred to two
inscriptions from the Temple, but there are other inscriptions
of a secular nature available for study today. Then there is
the coinage of the period with a good deal of interesting history preserved in an incidental way. Herod himself issued
coins in bronze, with the inscription in Greek, his symbols
being the pomegranate and leaves, the tripod and palms, the
eagle, the cornucopia, and three ears of barley. He was wise
enough to keep human figures off his coins since this would
have been a serious offense in the eyes of the Jews.

In the valley to the east of the present wall of Jerusalem is
a number of tombs bearing ancient names. An inscription on
one of them, known as the tomb of St. James, mentions several
members of the priestly order of Bene Hezir (I Chron. 24:15),
three of whom seem to have been high priests in the reign of
Herod.[15] The "Pyramid of Zacharias," and the "Tomb of
Jehoshaphat" belong to the same period, which Professor Albright holds to be the time of Herod.

Outside Judea there are the important remains of the Nabataeans, many of which were standing in the days of Herod,
just at the close of the Hasmonean era. We have seen how
Herod's father was friendly with these people and indeed
Herod spent some time with them in his youth. One of the
greatest of the kings of the Nabataeans was Aretas IV, who
ruled from about 9 B.C. till 40 A.D. It was he who did a great

15. W. F. Albright, op. cit., p. 157.

deal to modernize and adorn Petra, playing a similar role in his country to that of Herod in Judea. Archaeologists distinguish a classical Nabataean period, from the first century B.C. to the time of the Roman occupation in 106 A.D. This was well under way in Herod's day, but detailed discussion lies outside the scope of this book.

CONCLUSION

With the completion of our discussion of Herod we have ended our task, which was to follow the story of the Jews from the time when they returned from exile in Babylonia, until the dawn of the New Testament era, and to supplement this story with archaeological evidence bearing on it. The discussion has taken us outside Palestine a good deal, but in the nature of things we find our evidence wherever the Jews lived during these centuries. In any case, one never knows when archaeological material from almost anywhere in the East will throw light on the people of the Bible, since the contacts with Palestine were so numerous and so varied.

In the meantime it is worth observing that a period of Biblical history which for many Bible readers is practically closed, is not without a charm of its own. There is something exciting in building up the Biblical records with information from non-Biblical historians and from the thrilling discoveries of modern archaeology. It is very evident once again that the Biblical records have their roots firmly entrenched in general world history. Archaeological discovery supplements, explains, and corroborates the Biblical story at many points, and we are beginning to feel that an obscure period of Jewish history is already becoming brighter because of the many small, but significant, lights that pierce the darkness. The happy combination of the Biblical records, the non-Biblical histories, and the discoveries of the archaeologists has produced such splendid results to date that we are full of optimism that in the future this little known period of history will light up with a new glow.

Our story closes when the "fullness of time" had already come. There is useful archaeological evidence for the years 4 B.C. to 100 A.D., but that is a story which must be told in yet another volume.[16]

16. E. M. Blaiklock, *Out of the Earth* (Grand Rapids, 1957), gives a brief outline of some of the material available.

	BABYLONIAN, PERSIAN AND GREEK KINGS		THE JEWS
600	*BABYLONIAN KINGS* Nebuchadnezzar 605-562 Amel Marduk 562-560 Neriglissar 560-556 Nabonidus 556-539		586 Fall of Jerusalem
550			
	PERSIAN KINGS Cyrus 539-530 Cambyses 530-522 Darius 522-486		538 Edict of Cyrus 520 Haggai and Zechariah 516 Temple completed
500	Xerxes 486-465 Artaxerxes I 465-424		Esther 458 Ezra Malachi
			445 Nehemiah 432 Nehemiah recalled
450	Xerxes II 424-423 Darius II 423-404		
400			407 Elephantine Letter
	Artaxerxes II 404-358		
	Artaxerxes III 358-338 Arses 338-336 Darius III 336-331		
350	*GREEK KINGS*		
	Ptolemies	*Seleucids*	332 Jews fall under Greeks
	Ptolemy I 323-283		320 Ptolemies take control
300	Ptolemy II 283-246		Ptolemies in
	Ptolemy III 246-221	*Early Seleucid Kings*	
250			Palestine
	Ptolemy IV 221-203 Ptolemy V 203-181	Antiochus III 223-187	
200		Seleucus IV 187-175 Antiochus IV 175-163	198 Seleucids take Palestine 167 Pollution of Temple 166-160 Judas
		Antiochus V 163-162	164 Temple cleansed
	Later Ptolemaic Kings	Demetrius I 162-150	160-142 Jonathan 152 Jonathan High Priest
150		Balas 150-145 (Antiochus VI 145-142 (Demetrius II 145-139	142-134 Simon
		Antiochus VII 139-129	134-104 John Hyrcanus
		Seleucids continue	104-103 Aristobulus I 103-76 Alexander Jannaeus
100		with internal troubles till Roman conquest in 63 B.C.	
			76-67 Alexandra 67-63 Aristobulus II 63 Pompey takes Jerusalem 63-40 Hyrcanus II
50			
			40-37 Antigonus Mattathias
0			37- 4 Herod

INDEX OF SUBJECTS AND PERSONS

INDEX OF AUTHORS

INDEX OF BIBLE REFERENCES